Smart Start M[...] 102 Popular Weight Watchers Breakfast Recipes

Amelie Bright Lorelei

Copyright © 2024 Amelie Bright Lorelei
All rights reserved.
:

Contents

INTRODUCTION 8
1. Greek Yogurt Parfait 10
2. Scrambled Egg Whites with Spinach 11
3. Overnight Oats with Almond Butter 12
4. Avocado Toast with Poached Egg 13
5. Berry Protein Smoothie 15
6. Veggie Omelette 16
7. Whole Wheat Pancakes with Berries 17
8. Chia Seed Pudding with Berries 18
9. Apple Cinnamon Quinoa Porridge 20
10. Banana Walnut Muffins 21
11. Spinach and Feta Breakfast Quesadilla 22
12. Blueberry Almond Baked Oatmeal 24
13. Veggie and Egg Breakfast Burrito 25
14. Mixed Berry Smoothie Bowl 27
15. Cottage Cheese and Fruit Bowl 28
16. Peanut Butter and Banana Toast 29
17. Breakfast Stuffed Peppers 30
18. Spinach and Mushroom Breakfast Pizza 32
19. Oat Bran and Raspberry Muffins 33
20. Sweet Potato Hash with Turkey Sausage 35
21. Breakfast Egg and Veggie Muffins 36
22. Apple Cider Protein Pancakes 37
23. Quinoa and Black Bean Breakfast Bowl 39
24. Greek Yogurt and Honey Waffles 40
25. Green Breakfast Smoothie 42
26. Spinach and Cheese Breakfast Quesadilla 43
27. Baked Egg in Avocado 44

28. Almond Joy Protein Shake 45
29. Peanut Butter and Jelly Overnight Oats 47
30. Breakfast Quiche with Spinach and Tomatoes 48
31. Banana Nut Overnight Oats 49
32. Veggie Frittata with Goat Cheese 50
33. Blueberry Protein Pancakes 52
34. Breakfast Burrito Bowl 53
35. Egg White and Turkey Bacon Breakfast Sandwich 54
36. Raspberry Chia Pudding 56
37. Greek Yogurt and Mixed Berry Parfait 57
38. Spinach and Mushroom Egg White Omelette 59
39. Whole Wheat Pancakes with Cinnamon Apples 60
40. Breakfast Tacos with Salsa 62
41. Peanut Butter and Banana Protein Pancakes 63
42. Breakfast Stuffed Sweet Potatoes 64
43. Strawberry Almond Oatmeal 66
44. Egg White and Turkey Sausage Breakfast Wrap 67
45. Quinoa and Berry Breakfast Salad 69
46. Cinnamon Raisin Protein French Toast 70
47. Greek Yogurt and Granola Parfait 71
48. Spinach and Tomato Breakfast Quiche 73
49. Veggie Breakfast Skillet 74
50. Pumpkin Pie Protein Smoothie 76
51. Breakfast Sandwich with Turkey Sausage 77
52. Breakfast Chia Pudding with Berries 78
53. Whole Wheat Waffles with Fresh Berries 79
54. Oatmeal with Sliced Peaches 81
55. Veggie and Egg Breakfast Tostadas 82
56. Blueberry Almond Protein Pancakes 84

57. Breakfast Baked Potato 85
58. Greek Yogurt and Mango Parfait 86
59. Spinach and Feta Breakfast Strata.. 88
60. Cinnamon Apple Oatmeal 89
61. Breakfast Quesadilla with Turkey Bacon.................................... 90
62. Strawberry Banana Protein Smoothie 92
63. Peanut Butter and Chocolate Overnight Oats............................ 93
64. Breakfast Stuffed Bell Peppers... 94
65. Veggie and Egg Breakfast Muffins 96
66. Whole Wheat Pancakes with Mixed Berries.............................. 97
67. Breakfast Tacos with Avocado... 98
68. Caramelized Banana Protein Pancakes 100
69. Breakfast Salad with Poached Egg 101
70. Greek Yogurt and Berry Parfait... 103
71. Spinach and Tomato Breakfast Pizza.. 104
72. Blueberry Protein Waffles.. 105
73. Breakfast Burrito with Turkey Sausage.................................... 106
74. Breakfast Stuffed Mushrooms... 108
75. Peanut Butter and Jelly Protein Pancakes 109
76. Oatmeal with Sliced Strawberries 111
77. Veggie and Egg Breakfast Bowl.. 112
78. Breakfast Tostadas with Avocado 113
79. Cinnamon Raisin Protein French Toast................................... 115
80. Breakfast Quiche with Spinach and Turkey Sausage.............. 116
81. Raspberry Chia Pudding.. 117
82. Greek Yogurt and Honey Parfait... 119
83. Spinach and Feta Breakfast Quesadilla.................................... 120
84. Blueberry Almond Baked Oatmeal 121
85. Veggie and Egg Breakfast Burrito... 123

86. Mixed Berry Smoothie Bowl 124
87. Cottage Cheese and Fruit Bowl 125
88. Peanut Butter and Banana Toast 127
89. Breakfast Stuffed Peppers 128
90. Spinach and Mushroom Breakfast Pizza 129
91. Oat Bran and Raspberry Muffins 131
92. Sweet Potato Hash with Turkey Sausage 132
93. Breakfast Egg and Veggie Muffins 134
94. Apple Cider Protein Pancakes 135
95. Quinoa and Black Bean Breakfast Bowl 136
96. Greek Yogurt and Honey Waffles 138
97. Green Breakfast Smoothie 139
98. Spinach and Cheese Breakfast Quesadilla 140
99. Baked Egg in Avocado 142
100. Almond Joy Protein Shake 143
101. Peanut Butter and Jelly Overnight Oats 144
102. Breakfast Quiche with Spinach and Tomatoes 145
CONCLUSION 147

INTRODUCTION

Smart Start Mornings: 102 Popular Weight Watchers Breakfast Recipes"

Welcome to "Smart Start Mornings: 102 Popular Weight Watchers Breakfast Recipes," your essential companion to starting your day off right with delicious and nutritious breakfast options that align with the Weight Watchers program. This cookbook is designed to make your mornings easier, tastier, and healthier, whether you're aiming to lose weight or simply maintain a balanced lifestyle.

Breakfast is often hailed as the most important meal of the day, and with good reason. It sets the tone for your energy levels, mood, and cravings throughout the day. At Weight Watchers, we understand the significance of starting your day with smart choices that satisfy both your taste buds and your health goals. That's why we've curated this collection of 102 breakfast recipes that are not only flavorful and diverse but also mindful of your wellness journey.

In "Smart Start Mornings," you'll find a wide array of breakfast ideas that cater to various tastes and dietary preferences. From hearty and comforting classics to innovative and trendy options, each recipe is crafted with ingredients that support a balanced diet and are easy to incorporate into your daily routine. Whether you prefer quick and convenient meals for busy mornings or leisurely brunch ideas for weekends, there's something here to suit every occasion.

Our recipes are not just about counting calories or points—they're about enjoying food that fuels your body and enhances your well-being. Each recipe in this cookbook includes the SmartPoints values, so you can track your intake effortlessly and stay on track with your goals. We believe in the power of informed choices and the joy of cooking, and we've designed these recipes to inspire and empower you on your wellness journey.

As you explore "Smart Start Mornings," you'll discover tips and tricks for making the most of your breakfast routine. Whether you're new to the Weight Watchers program or a seasoned member looking for fresh ideas, this cookbook will become your go-to resource for starting your day on a deliciously healthy note.

We invite you to embrace a new approach to breakfast with "Smart Start Mornings: 102 Popular Weight Watchers Breakfast Recipes." Let this cookbook be your companion in creating mornings that are not only smart but also satisfying and full of flavor. Here's to making every breakfast a step towards a healthier, happier you!

1. Greek Yogurt Parfait

Start your day on a delicious and nutritious note with this Greek Yogurt Parfait, a perfect addition to your Weight Watchers breakfast repertoire. Packed with protein, fiber, and a burst of natural sweetness, this parfait is not only satisfying but also a guilt-free treat to kickstart your morning. Customize it with your favorite fruits and toppings to make it uniquely yours!

Serving: Serves 2
Preparation Time: 10 minutes
Ready Time: 10 minutes

Ingredients:
- 2 cups non-fat Greek yogurt
- 1 cup fresh mixed berries (strawberries, blueberries, raspberries)
- 1/2 cup granola (choose a low-sugar or sugar-free option for a healthier twist)
- 2 tablespoons honey or maple syrup (optional)
- 1/4 cup chopped nuts (almonds, walnuts, or pistachios)

Instructions:
1. In two serving glasses or bowls, start by layering 1/4 cup of Greek yogurt at the bottom.
2. Add a layer of mixed berries on top of the yogurt, evenly distributing the berries between the two servings.
3. Sprinkle 2 tablespoons of granola over the berries in each glass, creating a delightful crunch.
4. Drizzle 1 tablespoon of honey or maple syrup over each parfait if you desire a touch of sweetness.
5. Add another layer of Greek yogurt on top of the granola.
6. Finish by topping each parfait with the remaining mixed berries and a sprinkle of chopped nuts for added texture.
7. Serve immediately and enjoy the perfect balance of creamy yogurt, sweet berries, and crunchy granola.

Nutrition Information
(per serving):

- Calories: 250, Protein: 20g, Carbohydrates: 30g, Dietary Fiber: 5g, Sugars: 15g, Fat: 7g, Saturated Fat: 1g, Cholesterol: 5mg, Sodium: 80mg
Note: Nutrition Information may vary based on specific ingredients used.

2. Scrambled Egg Whites with Spinach

Start your day on a healthy note with our delightful recipe for Scrambled Egg Whites with Spinach. Packed with protein and nutrient-rich spinach, this breakfast option is not only delicious but also perfect for those following the Weight Watchers program. Say goodbye to the guilt and savor a satisfying meal that will keep you energized throughout the morning.

Serving: 2 servings
Preparation Time: 10 minutes
Ready Time: 15 minutes

Ingredients:
- 1 cup fresh spinach, chopped
- 8 egg whites
- 1/4 cup skim milk
- Salt and pepper to taste
- 1 tablespoon olive oil
- Optional: a sprinkle of feta cheese for garnish

Instructions:
1. Heat olive oil in a non-stick skillet over medium heat.
2. Add the chopped spinach to the skillet and sauté until wilted, about 2-3 minutes.
3. In a bowl, whisk together the egg whites, skim milk, salt, and pepper.
4. Pour the egg white mixture over the spinach in the skillet.
5. Gently scramble the eggs and spinach until the eggs are cooked through, about 5-7 minutes.
6. Optional: Sprinkle with feta cheese for an extra burst of flavor.
7. Remove from heat and serve immediately.

Nutrition Information:

Note: Nutrition Information is approximate and may vary based on specific ingredients used.
- Calories: 120 per serving, Protein: 20g, Fat: 3g, Carbohydrates: 3g, Fiber: 1g, Sugar: 1g, Sodium: 300mg

Enjoy a guilt-free breakfast that not only tastes delicious but also supports your wellness goals. Scrambled Egg Whites with Spinach is a wholesome and satisfying way to kickstart your day!

3. Overnight Oats with Almond Butter

Jumpstart your day with a nutritious and delicious breakfast that's perfect for anyone on the Weight Watchers journey. Our "Overnight Oats with Almond Butter" is not only a time-saver but also a delightful way to stay on track with your wellness goals. Packed with wholesome ingredients and the rich flavor of almond butter, this breakfast will keep you satisfied and energized throughout the morning.

Serving: 2 servings
Preparation Time: 10 minutes
Ready Time: Overnight (8 hours)

Ingredients:
- 1 cup old-fashioned rolled oats
- 1 cup unsweetened almond milk
- 2 tablespoons almond butter
- 1 tablespoon chia seeds
- 1 tablespoon maple syrup (optional, for sweetness)
- 1/2 teaspoon vanilla extract
- Pinch of salt
- Fresh berries and sliced almonds for topping (optional)

Instructions:
1. In a mixing bowl, combine the rolled oats, almond milk, almond butter, chia seeds, maple syrup (if using), vanilla extract, and a pinch of salt.
2. Stir the ingredients until well combined, ensuring the almond butter is evenly distributed throughout the mixture.
3. Divide the mixture into two jars or containers with lids.

4. Seal the jars and refrigerate overnight, allowing the oats to absorb the liquid and achieve a creamy consistency.
5. The next morning, give the oats a good stir and check the consistency. If desired, add a splash of almond milk to reach your preferred thickness.
6. Top the overnight oats with fresh berries and sliced almonds for an extra burst of flavor and texture.
7. Enjoy your hearty and satisfying breakfast guilt-free!

Nutrition Information:
Per serving (without optional toppings):
- Calories: 280, Protein: 8g, Fat: 13g, Carbohydrates: 33g, Fiber: 7g, Sugar: 2g, Sodium: 120mg
Note: Nutrition Information may vary based on specific ingredients used and optional toppings. Adjust quantities accordingly to meet your dietary preferences.

4. Avocado Toast with Poached Egg

Start your day on a healthy note with this delicious and nutritious Avocado Toast with Poached Egg. Packed with the goodness of creamy avocado and a perfectly poached egg, this breakfast recipe is not only satisfying but also a smart choice for those following the Weight Watchers program. The combination of wholesome ingredients makes it a filling and flavorful way to kickstart your morning while staying mindful of your wellness goals.

Serving: 2 servings
Preparation Time: 10 minutes
Ready Time: 15 minutes

Ingredients:
- 2 slices whole-grain bread (choose a lower-point option for Weight Watchers)
- 1 ripe avocado, peeled, pitted, and mashed
- 2 large eggs
- Salt and pepper to taste
- Red pepper flakes (optional, for added spice)
- Chopped fresh chives or parsley for garnish

Instructions:
1. Toast the Bread:
- Toast the slices of whole-grain bread until they reach your desired level of crispiness.
2. Prepare the Avocado:
- In a bowl, mash the ripe avocado with a fork until smooth. Season with a pinch of salt and pepper to taste.
3. Poach the Eggs:
- Bring a pot of water to a gentle simmer. Crack each egg into a small bowl.
- Create a gentle whirlpool in the simmering water by stirring it with a spoon. Carefully slide the eggs, one at a time, into the center of the whirlpool. Allow them to poach for about 3-4 minutes for a runny yolk or longer if you prefer a firmer yolk.
- Remove the poached eggs with a slotted spoon and place them on a paper towel to absorb excess water.
4. Assemble the Avocado Toast:
- Spread the mashed avocado evenly over each slice of toasted bread.
- Place a poached egg on top of the avocado on each slice.
5. Season and Garnish:
- Sprinkle salt and pepper over the poached eggs to taste. If you enjoy a bit of heat, add red pepper flakes.
- Garnish with chopped fresh chives or parsley for a burst of freshness.
6. Serve:
- Serve the Avocado Toast with Poached Egg immediately while the eggs are still warm.

Nutrition Information:
- Note: Nutritional values may vary based on specific bread and avocado used.
- Calories: Approximately 300 per serving, Protein: 12g, Carbohydrates: 25g, Dietary Fiber: 8g, Sugars: 2g, Fat: 18g, Saturated Fat: 3g, Cholesterol: 185mg, Sodium: 350mg

Start your day with a delicious and healthy breakfast that aligns with your Weight Watchers journey. This Avocado Toast with Poached Egg is a delightful way to fuel your body with the nutrients it needs without compromising on flavor.

5. Berry Protein Smoothie

Start your day on a deliciously healthy note with this Berry Protein Smoothie, a perfect addition to our collection of Popular Weight Watchers Breakfast Recipes. Packed with vibrant berries and a boost of protein, this smoothie is not only a tasty treat but also a great way to fuel your morning and stay on track with your weight loss goals.

Serving: 2 servings
Preparation Time: 10 minutes
Ready Time: 10 minutes

Ingredients:
- 1 cup frozen mixed berries (strawberries, blueberries, raspberries)
- 1 banana, peeled and sliced
- 1/2 cup non-fat Greek yogurt
- 1 scoop vanilla protein powder
- 1 tablespoon chia seeds
- 1 cup unsweetened almond milk
- 1 teaspoon honey (optional, for added sweetness)
- Ice cubes (optional)

Instructions:
1. In a blender, combine the frozen mixed berries, sliced banana, non-fat Greek yogurt, vanilla protein powder, chia seeds, and unsweetened almond milk.
2. If you prefer a sweeter taste, add honey to the blender.
3. Blend the ingredients on high speed until the mixture is smooth and creamy.
4. If you like your smoothie colder or thicker, you can add ice cubes and blend again until well combined.
5. Pour the smoothie into glasses and garnish with a few extra berries or a slice of banana if desired.
6. Serve immediately and enjoy this nutritious and satisfying Berry Protein Smoothie to kickstart your day.

Nutrition Information
(per serving):
- Calories: 220, Protein: 20g, Carbohydrates: 32g, Fiber: 8g, Sugar: 15g, Fat: 4g, Saturated Fat: 0.5g, Cholesterol: 5mg, Sodium: 120mg

Feel free to customize the recipe based on your preferences and dietary needs. Cheers to a delicious and healthy start to your day!

6. Veggie Omelette

Start your day on a healthy note with this delightful Veggie Omelette, a perfect addition to our collection of Popular Weight Watchers Breakfast Recipes. Packed with vibrant vegetables and protein-rich eggs, this dish is not only delicious but also a smart choice for those watching their weight. Enjoy a flavorful and satisfying breakfast that won't compromise your commitment to a balanced lifestyle.

Serving: Serves 2
Preparation Time: 15 minutes
Ready Time: 20 minutes

Ingredients:
- 4 large eggs
- 1/4 cup skim milk
- Salt and pepper to taste
- 1 tablespoon olive oil
- 1/2 cup diced bell peppers (mix of red, green, and yellow)
- 1/2 cup diced tomatoes
- 1/4 cup diced red onion
- 1/4 cup chopped spinach
- 1/4 cup diced mushrooms
- 1/4 cup reduced-fat feta cheese, crumbled
- 1 tablespoon fresh chives, chopped (for garnish)

Instructions:
1. In a bowl, whisk together the eggs, skim milk, salt, and pepper until well combined.
2. Heat olive oil in a non-stick skillet over medium heat.
3. Add bell peppers, tomatoes, red onion, spinach, and mushrooms to the skillet. Sauté the vegetables until they are tender but still crisp, about 3-4 minutes.
4. Pour the whisked egg mixture over the sautéed vegetables in the skillet.

5. Allow the eggs to set slightly around the edges. With a spatula, gently lift the edges, tilting the skillet to let the uncooked egg flow to the edges.
6. Sprinkle feta cheese evenly over the omelette.
7. Once the edges are set and the center is still slightly runny, carefully fold the omelette in half.
8. Continue cooking for an additional 1-2 minutes or until the eggs are fully cooked and the cheese is melted.
9. Slide the Veggie Omelette onto a plate and garnish with fresh chives.
10. Serve hot and enjoy a delicious, satisfying breakfast!

Nutrition Information:
Per Serving
- Calories: 220, Total Fat: 14g, Saturated Fat: 4g, Cholesterol: 372mg, Sodium: 320mg, Total Carbohydrates: 9g, Dietary Fiber: 2g, Sugars: 5g, Protein: 16g

Note: Nutrition Information is approximate and may vary based on specific ingredients used. Adjustments can be made based on personal preferences and dietary needs.

7. Whole Wheat Pancakes with Berries

Start your day on a delicious and nutritious note with our Whole Wheat Pancakes with Berries—a perfect addition to your Popular Weight Watchers Breakfast Recipes collection. These wholesome pancakes combine the hearty goodness of whole wheat with the vibrant sweetness of fresh berries, creating a breakfast treat that's both satisfying and figure-friendly.

Serving: Makes 4 servings (3 pancakes per serving)
Preparation Time: 15 minutes
Ready Time: 25 minutes

Ingredients:
- 1 cup whole wheat flour
- 1 tablespoon sugar
- 1 teaspoon baking powder
- 1/2 teaspoon baking soda
- 1/4 teaspoon salt

- 1 cup buttermilk
- 1 large egg
- 2 tablespoons unsalted butter, melted
- 1 teaspoon vanilla extract
- 1 cup mixed berries (blueberries, raspberries, strawberries)

Instructions:
1. In a large mixing bowl, whisk together the whole wheat flour, sugar, baking powder, baking soda, and salt.
2. In a separate bowl, whisk together the buttermilk, egg, melted butter, and vanilla extract.
3. Pour the wet ingredients into the dry ingredients and stir until just combined. Be careful not to overmix; a few lumps are okay.
4. Heat a griddle or non-stick skillet over medium heat. Lightly coat with cooking spray or a small amount of butter.
5. Pour 1/4 cup of batter onto the griddle for each pancake. Cook until bubbles form on the surface, then flip and cook until the other side is golden brown.
6. Repeat until all the batter is used, keeping the cooked pancakes warm in a low oven if needed.
7. Serve the pancakes topped with a generous handful of mixed berries.

Nutrition Information
(per serving):
- Calories: 250, Protein: 8g, Fat: 8g, Carbohydrates: 38g, Fiber: 6g, Sugars: 9g, Sodium: 450mg

Enjoy these guilt-free Whole Wheat Pancakes with Berries as a delicious and satisfying breakfast option that aligns perfectly with your weight-conscious lifestyle.

8. Chia Seed Pudding with Berries

Chia seed pudding with berries is a delightful and nutritious breakfast option, especially for those on a Weight Watchers journey. It's a fantastic way to start your day with a burst of flavors and the health benefits of chia seeds and fresh berries. This recipe is not only delicious but also incredibly simple to prepare, making it a perfect addition to your morning routine.

Serving: 2 servings
Preparation time: 5 minutes
Ready time: 4 hours (Chilling time)

Ingredients:
- 1/4 cup chia seeds
- 1 cup unsweetened almond milk (or any preferred milk)
- 1 tablespoon maple syrup or honey (optional, for sweetness)
- 1/2 teaspoon vanilla extract
- 1 cup mixed berries (strawberries, blueberries, raspberries)
- Fresh mint leaves for garnish (optional)

Instructions:
1. In a mixing bowl, combine the chia seeds, almond milk, sweetener (if using), and vanilla extract. Stir well to ensure the chia seeds are evenly distributed.
2. Let the mixture sit for 5 minutes and then stir it again to prevent clumping.
3. Cover the bowl and refrigerate for at least 4 hours or preferably overnight to allow the chia seeds to absorb the liquid and form a pudding-like consistency.
4. Before serving, give the chia pudding a good stir to break up any clumps that may have formed. If the pudding is too thick, you can add a splash of almond milk to reach your desired consistency.
5. Wash and prepare the mixed berries. You can slice larger berries like strawberries if desired.
6. Divide the chia seed pudding into serving bowls or glasses.
7. Top the pudding with the mixed berries and garnish with fresh mint leaves if using.
8. Serve chilled and enjoy this delightful and nutritious breakfast!

Nutrition Information
(per serving, excluding sweetener):
- Calories: 150, Total Fat: 7g, Saturated Fat: 0.5g, Cholesterol: 0mg, Sodium: 80mg
- Total Carbohydrate: 18g, Dietary Fiber: 10g, Sugars: 4g, Protein: 5g

Remember, feel free to adjust the sweetness level according to your preference or dietary needs. This chia seed pudding with berries is not just a treat for your taste buds but also a great way to kickstart your day with a dose of healthy nutrients!

9. Apple Cinnamon Quinoa Porridge

Start your day on a nutritious note with this delightful Apple Cinnamon Quinoa Porridge. Packed with the wholesome goodness of quinoa, the sweetness of apples, and the comforting warmth of cinnamon, this breakfast dish is not only delicious but also friendly for those following the Weight Watchers program.

Serving: This recipe serves 4.
Preparation Time: Preparation takes approximately 5 minutes.
Ready Time: The porridge will be ready in about 25 minutes.

Ingredients:
- 1 cup quinoa, rinsed
- 2 cups unsweetened almond milk
- 2 cups water
- 2 medium apples, peeled, cored, and diced
- 2 tablespoons pure maple syrup or sweetener of choice
- 1 teaspoon ground cinnamon
- 1/4 teaspoon ground nutmeg
- Pinch of salt
- Optional toppings: sliced almonds, chopped walnuts, additional diced apples, a drizzle of honey or more maple syrup

Instructions:
1. Rinse the quinoa thoroughly under cold water using a fine mesh strainer.
2. In a medium-sized saucepan, combine the rinsed quinoa, almond milk, water, diced apples, maple syrup, cinnamon, nutmeg, and a pinch of salt.
3. Bring the mixture to a gentle boil over medium heat.
4. Once boiling, reduce the heat to low, cover the saucepan, and let the porridge simmer for about 20 minutes or until the quinoa is tender and the liquid is absorbed. Stir occasionally.
5. Once cooked, remove the saucepan from the heat and let it sit, covered, for 5 minutes to allow the flavors to meld.

6. Give the porridge a good stir before serving. If desired, top each serving with sliced almonds, chopped walnuts, additional diced apples, or a drizzle of honey or maple syrup.

Nutrition Information
(per serving):
- Calories: 240, Total Fat: 4g, Saturated Fat: 0.3g, Cholesterol: 0mg, Sodium: 90mg
- Total Carbohydrate: 45g, Dietary Fiber: 6g, Sugars: 15g, Protein: 6g
- WW SmartPoints (Blue/Purple): 6 points

10. Banana Walnut Muffins

Start your day on a delicious and nutritious note with our Banana Walnut Muffins—a perfect addition to your collection of Popular Weight Watchers Breakfast Recipes. These moist and flavorful muffins strike the ideal balance between wholesome ingredients and delightful taste. Packed with the goodness of bananas and the crunch of walnuts, these muffins are a guilt-free way to satisfy your morning cravings.

Serving: Makes 12 muffins
Preparation Time: 15 minutes
Ready Time: 30 minutes

Ingredients:
- 2 ripe bananas, mashed
- 1/2 cup unsweetened applesauce
- 1/3 cup honey or maple syrup
- 1 large egg
- 1 teaspoon vanilla extract
- 1 1/2 cups whole wheat flour
- 1 teaspoon baking soda
- 1/2 teaspoon baking powder
- 1/2 teaspoon cinnamon
- 1/4 teaspoon salt
- 1/2 cup chopped walnuts

Instructions:

1. Preheat your oven to 350°F (175°C). Line a muffin tin with paper liners or lightly grease with cooking spray.
2. In a large bowl, combine the mashed bananas, applesauce, honey (or maple syrup), egg, and vanilla extract. Mix well until smooth.
3. In a separate bowl, whisk together the whole wheat flour, baking soda, baking powder, cinnamon, and salt.
4. Gradually add the dry ingredients to the banana mixture, stirring until just combined. Be careful not to overmix.
5. Gently fold in the chopped walnuts, reserving a few for topping.
6. Spoon the batter into the prepared muffin cups, filling each about two-thirds full. Top each muffin with a sprinkle of the reserved chopped walnuts.
7. Bake in the preheated oven for 18-20 minutes or until a toothpick inserted into the center comes out clean.
8. Allow the muffins to cool in the tin for 5 minutes before transferring them to a wire rack to cool completely.

Nutrition Information:
Per Serving (1 muffin):
- Calories: 140, Total Fat: 4g, Saturated Fat: 0.5g, Cholesterol: 15mg, Sodium: 150mg, Total Carbohydrates: 26g, Dietary Fiber: 3g, Sugars: 12g, Protein: 3g

These Banana Walnut Muffins are not only a tasty breakfast treat but also a smart choice for those mindful of their Weight Watchers points. Enjoy the delightful blend of flavors while keeping your wellness goals on track!

11. Spinach and Feta Breakfast Quesadilla

Start your day on a nutritious and delicious note with our Spinach and Feta Breakfast Quesadilla. Packed with vibrant flavors, this Weight Watchers-friendly breakfast is the perfect way to kickstart your morning while keeping your wellness goals in check. The combination of wholesome spinach, creamy feta, and savory seasonings will make this quesadilla a breakfast favorite.

Serving: Makes 2 quesadillas
Preparation Time: 15 minutes

Ready Time: 20 minutes

Ingredients:
- 4 whole wheat tortillas (8-inch size)
- 2 cups fresh baby spinach, chopped
- 1 cup reduced-fat feta cheese, crumbled
- 1 medium tomato, diced
- 1/4 cup red onion, finely chopped
- 1 teaspoon olive oil
- 1/2 teaspoon garlic powder
- 1/2 teaspoon dried oregano
- Salt and pepper to taste
- Cooking spray

Instructions:
1. Prepare the Filling:
- In a skillet, heat olive oil over medium heat. Add chopped spinach and cook until wilted, about 2-3 minutes. Season with garlic powder, dried oregano, salt, and pepper.
- Remove the skillet from heat and set aside the spinach mixture.
2. Assemble the Quesadillas:
- Lay out the whole wheat tortillas on a clean surface.
- Divide the cooked spinach evenly among two tortillas, spreading it evenly over one half of each tortilla.
- Sprinkle crumbled feta cheese over the spinach on each tortilla.
- Add diced tomatoes and chopped red onions on top of the feta.
3. Fold and Cook:
- Fold the empty half of each tortilla over the filling, creating a half-moon shape.
- Heat a non-stick skillet over medium heat and coat with cooking spray.
- Place the quesadillas in the skillet and cook for 2-3 minutes per side, or until the tortillas are golden brown and the cheese is melted.
4. Serve:
- Remove from the skillet and let them cool for a minute before slicing each quesadilla into halves.

Nutrition Information:
Per Serving (1 quesadilla)

- Calories: 320, Protein: 15g, Carbohydrates: 40g, Dietary Fiber: 8g, Sugars: 4g, Total Fat: 12g, Saturated Fat: 5g, Cholesterol: 20mg, Sodium: 650mg

These Spinach and Feta Breakfast Quesadillas are not only a tasty and satisfying breakfast option but also a nutritious choice to keep you fueled throughout the day. Enjoy guilt-free indulgence while staying on track with your Weight Watchers journey.

12. Blueberry Almond Baked Oatmeal

Start your day on a delicious and healthy note with our Blueberry Almond Baked Oatmeal, a perfect addition to your Popular Weight Watchers Breakfast Recipes collection. Packed with wholesome ingredients and bursting with the natural sweetness of blueberries, this baked oatmeal is a delightful and satisfying way to fuel your morning.

Serving: Serves 6
Preparation Time: 15 minutes
Ready Time: 45 minutes

Ingredients:
- 2 cups old-fashioned oats
- 1/2 cup slivered almonds
- 1 teaspoon baking powder
- 1/2 teaspoon cinnamon
- 1/4 teaspoon salt
- 1 1/2 cups unsweetened almond milk (or your choice of milk)
- 1/4 cup pure maple syrup
- 2 tablespoons almond butter
- 1 large egg
- 1 teaspoon vanilla extract
- 1 1/2 cups fresh or frozen blueberries

Instructions:
1. Preheat your oven to 350°F (175°C). Grease a baking dish with non-stick cooking spray.
2. In a large bowl, combine the oats, slivered almonds, baking powder, cinnamon, and salt. Mix well.

3. In a separate bowl, whisk together the almond milk, maple syrup, almond butter, egg, and vanilla extract until smooth and well combined.
4. Pour the wet ingredients into the bowl with the dry ingredients and stir until everything is evenly coated.
5. Gently fold in the blueberries, ensuring they are evenly distributed throughout the mixture.
6. Transfer the oatmeal mixture to the prepared baking dish, spreading it out evenly.
7. Bake in the preheated oven for 30-35 minutes or until the edges are golden brown and a toothpick inserted into the center comes out clean.
8. Allow the baked oatmeal to cool for a few minutes before slicing it into squares.

Nutrition Information:
(Per Serving)
- Calories: 280, Total Fat: 12g, Saturated Fat: 1g, Trans Fat: 0g, Cholesterol: 31mg, Sodium: 147mg, Total Carbohydrates: 37g, Dietary Fiber: 6g, Sugars: 12g, Protein: 8g

This Blueberry Almond Baked Oatmeal is not only a flavorful way to start your day but also a smart choice for those keeping an eye on their Weight Watchers points. Enjoy the wholesome goodness and delicious taste without compromising your wellness goals.

13. Veggie and Egg Breakfast Burrito

Start your day on a healthy and delicious note with this Veggie and Egg Breakfast Burrito, a perfect addition to your weight-conscious breakfast routine. Packed with nutritious vegetables and protein-rich eggs, this burrito will keep you satisfied and energized throughout the morning. It's a flavorful and satisfying choice for anyone looking to enjoy a tasty breakfast while keeping an eye on their weight.

Serving: Serves 2
Preparation Time: 15 minutes
Ready Time: 20 minutes

Ingredients:
- 4 whole wheat or low-carb tortillas

- 4 large eggs
- 1 cup diced bell peppers (assorted colors)
- 1 cup diced tomatoes
- 1/2 cup diced red onion
- 1/2 cup chopped fresh spinach
- 1/2 cup shredded reduced-fat cheddar cheese
- 1 teaspoon olive oil
- 1/2 teaspoon garlic powder
- Salt and pepper to taste
- Salsa and Greek yogurt for serving (optional)

Instructions:
1. Prepare the Vegetables:
- In a skillet, heat olive oil over medium heat. Add diced red onion, bell peppers, and tomatoes. Sauté until the vegetables are tender, about 5 minutes.
2. Scramble the Eggs:
- Push the sautéed vegetables to one side of the skillet. Crack the eggs into the empty side and scramble them until just set. Mix the eggs with the sautéed vegetables.
3. Add Spinach and Cheese:
- Stir in the chopped spinach, garlic powder, salt, and pepper. Cook for an additional 1-2 minutes until the spinach wilts and the ingredients are well combined. Sprinkle shredded cheddar cheese over the mixture and let it melt.
4. Warm the Tortillas:
- In a separate skillet or directly on a gas flame, warm each tortilla for about 10 seconds on each side until pliable.
5. Assemble the Burritos:
- Divide the egg and vegetable mixture evenly among the tortillas. Fold in the sides and roll up each tortilla to create a burrito.
6. Serve:
- Optionally, serve with salsa and a dollop of Greek yogurt for added flavor.

Nutrition Information:
(Per Serving)
- Calories: 300, Protein: 18g, Carbohydrates: 26g, Dietary Fiber: 6g, Sugars: 4g, Total Fat: 14g, Saturated Fat: 5g, Cholesterol: 370mg, Sodium: 450mg

- Vitamin D: 15%
- Calcium: 20%
- Iron: 15%
- Potassium: 25%

Enjoy this Veggie and Egg Breakfast Burrito guilt-free, as it not only satisfies your taste buds but also supports your weight-conscious lifestyle.

14. Mixed Berry Smoothie Bowl

Start your day on a deliciously healthy note with our Mixed Berry Smoothie Bowl! Packed with vibrant flavors and nutritional goodness, this breakfast recipe is a perfect choice for those following the Weight Watchers program. Bursting with the natural sweetness of mixed berries, this smoothie bowl is not only satisfying but also a delightful way to kickstart your morning routine. With a harmonious blend of ingredients, it's a guilt-free treat that will keep you energized and on track with your wellness goals.

Serving: This recipe serves 2.
Preparation Time: 10 minutes
Ready Time: 10 minutes

Ingredients:
- 1 cup frozen mixed berries (strawberries, blueberries, raspberries)
- 1 ripe banana
- 1/2 cup non-fat Greek yogurt
- 1/2 cup unsweetened almond milk
- 1 tablespoon chia seeds
- 1 tablespoon honey (optional, for added sweetness)
- 1/2 teaspoon vanilla extract
- Ice cubes (optional, for a thicker consistency)
- Fresh berries and granola for topping

Instructions:
1. In a blender, combine the frozen mixed berries, ripe banana, Greek yogurt, almond milk, chia seeds, honey (if using), and vanilla extract.

2. Blend the ingredients on high speed until smooth and creamy. If you prefer a thicker consistency, add ice cubes and blend again until well combined.
3. Pour the smoothie mixture into bowls.
4. Top the smoothie bowls with fresh berries and granola for added texture and flavor.
5. Serve immediately and enjoy your nutritious Mixed Berry Smoothie Bowl!

Nutrition Information:
Per Serving (without honey):
- Calories: 180, Protein: 8g, Carbohydrates: 38g, Dietary Fiber: 7g, Sugars: 19g, Fat: 2g, Saturated Fat: 0g, Cholesterol: 0mg, Sodium: 80mg
Note: Nutrition Information may vary based on specific brands and quantities of ingredients used.

15. Cottage Cheese and Fruit Bowl

Start your day on a delicious and nutritious note with this Cottage Cheese and Fruit Bowl—a perfect addition to your Popular Weight Watchers Breakfast Recipes. Packed with protein, vitamins, and a burst of natural sweetness, this breakfast bowl not only satisfies your taste buds but also supports your wellness goals. It's a delightful combination of creamy cottage cheese and vibrant fresh fruits that will leave you feeling energized and ready to tackle the day.

Serving: Serves 2
Preparation Time: 15 minutes
Ready Time: 15 minutes

Ingredients:
- 1 cup low-fat cottage cheese
- 1 cup strawberries, hulled and sliced
- 1 cup blueberries
- 1 medium banana, sliced
- 1 tablespoon honey (optional)
- 2 tablespoons chopped nuts (almonds, walnuts, or your choice)
- Fresh mint leaves for garnish

Instructions:
1. In a mixing bowl, spoon out the low-fat cottage cheese, ensuring a creamy base for your fruit bowl.
2. Add the sliced strawberries, blueberries, and banana to the cottage cheese. These colorful fruits not only add sweetness but also contribute essential vitamins and antioxidants.
3. Gently toss the fruits and cottage cheese together, ensuring an even distribution.
4. If you have a sweet tooth, drizzle a tablespoon of honey over the fruit and cheese mixture. This step is optional and can be adjusted based on your taste preferences.
5. Sprinkle the chopped nuts over the top for a satisfying crunch and an extra dose of healthy fats.
6. Divide the mixture into two serving bowls.
7. Garnish each bowl with fresh mint leaves for a burst of flavor and a visually appealing touch.
8. Your Cottage Cheese and Fruit Bowl is now ready to be enjoyed!

Nutrition Information
(per serving):
- Calories: 250, Protein: 18g, Carbohydrates: 35g, Dietary Fiber: 6g, Sugars: 22g, Fat: 6g, Saturated Fat: 1.5g, Cholesterol: 10mg, Sodium: 300mg
Note: Nutrition Information may vary based on specific ingredients used and can be adjusted based on individual dietary needs.

16. Peanut Butter and Banana Toast

Start your day on a delicious and nutritious note with our Peanut Butter and Banana Toast—a delightful twist to your morning routine. This weight watchers-friendly breakfast is not only satisfying but also a perfect balance of flavors. The creamy peanut butter pairs harmoniously with the sweetness of ripe bananas, creating a wholesome treat that will keep you energized throughout the day.

Serving: 2 servings
Preparation Time: 5 minutes

Ready Time: 7 minutes

Ingredients:
- 4 slices whole-grain bread
- 4 tablespoons natural peanut butter (unsweetened)
- 2 ripe bananas, thinly sliced
- 1 tablespoon honey (optional)
- Pinch of cinnamon (optional)

Instructions:
1. Toast the Bread: Place the slices of whole-grain bread in a toaster or toaster oven until they reach your desired level of crispiness.
2. Spread Peanut Butter: While the bread is still warm, spread 1 tablespoon of natural peanut butter onto each slice, ensuring an even layer.
3. Add Banana Slices: Arrange the thinly sliced bananas on top of the peanut butter-covered toast. Ensure an even distribution for a balanced bite.
4. Optional Sweetness: Drizzle a touch of honey over the banana slices for added sweetness. If you like, sprinkle a pinch of cinnamon for a warm, aromatic flavor.
5. Serve and Enjoy: Your Peanut Butter and Banana Toast is now ready to be enjoyed! Pair it with a cup of your favorite morning beverage for a satisfying and wholesome breakfast.

Nutrition Information
(per serving):
- Calories: 280, Total Fat: 12g, Saturated Fat: 2g, Cholesterol: 0mg, Sodium: 220mg, Total Carbohydrates: 38g, Dietary Fiber: 6g, Sugars: 14g, Protein: 8g

Note: Nutrition Information is approximate and may vary based on specific ingredients used. Adjustments can be made to fit individual dietary needs.

17. Breakfast Stuffed Peppers

Start your day on a delicious and healthy note with these Breakfast Stuffed Peppers! Packed with vibrant flavors and nutritious ingredients, this recipe is a perfect addition to your weight watchers' breakfast repertoire. The combination of colorful bell peppers, savory turkey sausage, and eggs creates a satisfying and low-point meal that will keep you energized throughout the morning.

Serving: Serves: 4
Preparation Time: Prep Time: 15 minutes
Ready Time: Ready in: 35 minutes

Ingredients:
- 4 large bell peppers, halved and seeds removed
- 1 pound lean turkey sausage, crumbled
- 1 cup cherry tomatoes, diced
- 1/2 cup red onion, finely chopped
- 1 cup spinach, chopped
- 1 teaspoon olive oil
- 8 large eggs
- Salt and pepper to taste
- 1/2 cup reduced-fat shredded cheddar cheese
- Fresh parsley for garnish (optional)

Instructions:
1. Preheat your oven to 375°F (190°C).
2. In a large skillet, heat the olive oil over medium heat. Add the turkey sausage and cook until browned, breaking it apart with a spoon as it cooks.
3. Add the red onion to the skillet and sauté until softened, about 3 minutes.
4. Stir in the cherry tomatoes and spinach, cooking until the spinach wilts and the tomatoes release their juices.
5. Place the bell pepper halves in a baking dish, cut side up.
6. Spoon the sausage and vegetable mixture evenly into each pepper half.
7. Carefully crack an egg into each pepper half, ensuring not to break the yolk.
8. Season each pepper with salt and pepper to taste.
9. Sprinkle the shredded cheddar cheese over the eggs.
10. Bake in the preheated oven for 20-25 minutes or until the egg whites are set, and the yolks are still slightly runny.
11. Garnish with fresh parsley if desired.

12. Serve warm and enjoy your delicious and satisfying Breakfast Stuffed Peppers!

Nutrition Information:
Per serving:
- Calories: 320, Total Fat: 15g, Saturated Fat: 5g, Cholesterol: 380mg, Sodium: 650mg, Total Carbohydrates: 15g, Dietary Fiber: 4g, Sugars: 7g, Protein: 28g

Note: Nutrition Information is approximate and may vary based on specific ingredients used.

18. Spinach and Mushroom Breakfast Pizza

Start your day with a burst of flavor and nutrition with this delightful Spinach and Mushroom Breakfast Pizza. Packed with wholesome ingredients, this recipe is not only delicious but also fits seamlessly into your Weight Watchers plan. The combination of fresh spinach, savory mushrooms, and a perfectly cooked egg creates a breakfast experience that's both satisfying and guilt-free.

Serving: Makes 4 servings
Preparation Time: 15 minutes
Ready Time: 25 minutes

Ingredients:
- 1 pound whole wheat pizza dough
- 1 cup part-skim mozzarella cheese, shredded
- 1 cup fresh spinach, chopped
- 1 cup mushrooms, sliced
- 4 large eggs
- 1 teaspoon olive oil
- 1 teaspoon garlic powder
- Salt and pepper to taste
- Optional: red pepper flakes for a spicy kick

Instructions:
1. Preheat Oven: Preheat your oven to 425°F (220°C).

2. Prepare Dough: Roll out the whole wheat pizza dough on a lightly floured surface, creating a thin crust. Place the rolled-out dough on a pizza stone or a baking sheet lined with parchment paper.

3. Saute Spinach and Mushrooms: In a skillet over medium heat, add olive oil. Sauté the sliced mushrooms until they are tender, and then add the chopped spinach. Cook until the spinach wilts. Season with garlic powder, salt, and pepper. Set aside.

4. Assemble Pizza: Spread the sautéed spinach and mushrooms evenly over the pizza dough. Sprinkle shredded mozzarella on top.

5. Create Wells for Eggs: Using the back of a spoon, make four wells in the pizza toppings. Carefully crack an egg into each well.

6. Bake: Transfer the pizza to the preheated oven and bake for 15-20 minutes or until the egg whites are set, and the yolks are still slightly runny.

7. Optional Spicy Kick: If you enjoy a bit of heat, sprinkle red pepper flakes over the pizza before serving.

8. Serve: Once the eggs are cooked to your liking, remove the pizza from the oven. Allow it to cool for a few minutes before slicing.

Nutrition Information:
(Per Serving)
- Calories: 350, Protein: 18g, Carbohydrates: 40g, Fiber: 6g, Sugars: 3g, Fat: 14g, Saturated Fat: 5g, Cholesterol: 195mg, Sodium: 550mg

This Spinach and Mushroom Breakfast Pizza is not only a delightful way to start your day but also a tasty addition to your Weight Watchers journey. Enjoy a guilt-free and satisfying breakfast that won't compromise your wellness goals.

19. Oat Bran and Raspberry Muffins

Start your day on a healthy and delicious note with these Oat Bran and Raspberry Muffins. Packed with fiber-rich oat bran and the vibrant sweetness of raspberries, these muffins are a delightful treat that won't compromise your commitment to a balanced breakfast. Created with Weight Watchers principles in mind, these muffins are a smart choice for those looking to kickstart their day with a tasty and nutritious breakfast.

Serving: Makes 12 muffins

Preparation Time: 15 minutes
Ready Time: 30 minutes

Ingredients:
- 1 cup oat bran
- 1 cup whole wheat flour
- 1/2 cup brown sugar, packed
- 1 teaspoon baking powder
- 1/2 teaspoon baking soda
- 1/4 teaspoon salt
- 1 cup non-fat Greek yogurt
- 2 large eggs
- 1/4 cup unsweetened applesauce
- 1 teaspoon vanilla extract
- 1 cup fresh raspberries

Instructions:
1. Preheat your oven to 375°F (190°C) and line a muffin tin with paper liners.
2. In a large mixing bowl, combine the oat bran, whole wheat flour, brown sugar, baking powder, baking soda, and salt. Mix well to ensure even distribution of dry ingredients.
3. In a separate bowl, whisk together the Greek yogurt, eggs, applesauce, and vanilla extract until smooth.
4. Pour the wet ingredients into the dry ingredients and gently fold until just combined. Be careful not to overmix; a few lumps are okay.
5. Gently fold in the fresh raspberries, ensuring they are evenly distributed throughout the batter.
6. Spoon the batter into the prepared muffin tin, filling each cup about two-thirds full.
7. Bake in the preheated oven for 15-18 minutes or until a toothpick inserted into the center of a muffin comes out clean.
8. Allow the muffins to cool in the tin for 5 minutes before transferring them to a wire rack to cool completely.

Nutrition Information:
Per Serving (1 muffin):
- Calories: 120, Total Fat: 1g, Saturated Fat: 0g, Cholesterol: 25mg, Sodium: 120mg, Total Carbohydrates: 24g, Dietary Fiber: 4g, Sugars: 8g, Protein: 5g

These Oat Bran and Raspberry Muffins make for a satisfying and guilt-free breakfast option, perfect for those following the Weight Watchers program. Enjoy the combination of hearty oat bran and the burst of flavor from fresh raspberries in every bite!

20. Sweet Potato Hash with Turkey Sausage

Start your day on a delicious and nutritious note with our Sweet Potato Hash with Turkey Sausage—a satisfying breakfast option that won't derail your weight loss journey. Packed with wholesome ingredients and bursting with flavors, this hearty dish is a perfect addition to your collection of Popular Weight Watchers Breakfast Recipes. With a balance of lean turkey sausage, vibrant sweet potatoes, and a medley of aromatic spices, this hash is a tasty way to kickstart your morning while keeping you on track with your wellness goals.

Serving: Serves 4
Preparation Time: 15 minutes
Ready Time: 30 minutes

Ingredients:
- 2 medium sweet potatoes, peeled and diced into 1/2-inch cubes
- 1 pound lean turkey sausage, casings removed
- 1 onion, finely chopped
- 1 bell pepper, diced
- 2 cloves garlic, minced
- 1 teaspoon smoked paprika
- 1/2 teaspoon ground cumin
- Salt and pepper to taste
- 1 tablespoon olive oil
- Fresh parsley, chopped (for garnish)

Instructions:
1. In a large skillet, heat olive oil over medium heat. Add diced sweet potatoes and cook until they begin to soften, about 8-10 minutes, stirring occasionally.

2. Add the lean turkey sausage to the skillet, breaking it apart with a spatula. Cook until the sausage is browned and cooked through, about 5-7 minutes.
3. Stir in the chopped onion, bell pepper, and minced garlic. Sauté until the vegetables are tender, about 5 minutes.
4. Sprinkle smoked paprika, ground cumin, salt, and pepper over the mixture. Stir well to combine, allowing the flavors to meld for another 2-3 minutes.
5. Once the sweet potatoes are fully cooked and slightly crispy, and the sausage and vegetables are well incorporated, remove the skillet from heat.
6. Garnish with freshly chopped parsley for a burst of freshness and color.

Nutrition Information:
Per serving:
- Calories: 320, Protein: 20g, Carbohydrates: 25g, Dietary Fiber: 4g, Sugars: 6g, Fat: 16g, Saturated Fat: 4g, Cholesterol: 60mg, Sodium: 680mg

Start your day with this flavorful Sweet Potato Hash with Turkey Sausage and embrace a breakfast that not only tastes delightful but also aligns with your weight watchers goals.

21. Breakfast Egg and Veggie Muffins

Start your day on a healthy and delicious note with these Breakfast Egg and Veggie Muffins. Packed with protein and loaded with colorful vegetables, these muffins are not only a treat for your taste buds but also a smart choice for those following the Weight Watchers program. Easy to make and perfectly portioned, these muffins are a great addition to your collection of popular Weight Watchers breakfast recipes.

Serving: Makes 12 muffins
Preparation Time: 15 minutes
Ready Time: 35 minutes

Ingredients:
- 8 large eggs

- 1/4 cup skim milk
- 1/2 teaspoon salt
- 1/4 teaspoon black pepper
- 1 cup diced bell peppers (assorted colors)
- 1/2 cup diced red onion
- 1/2 cup diced tomatoes
- 1/2 cup chopped spinach
- 1/4 cup finely chopped fresh parsley
- 1/2 cup shredded reduced-fat cheddar cheese

Instructions:
1. Preheat your oven to 350°F (175°C). Grease a muffin tin or line it with paper liners.
2. In a large bowl, whisk together the eggs, skim milk, salt, and black pepper until well combined.
3. Add the diced bell peppers, red onion, tomatoes, spinach, and fresh parsley to the egg mixture. Stir in the shredded cheddar cheese and mix until all ingredients are evenly distributed.
4. Pour the egg and veggie mixture into the prepared muffin tin, dividing it evenly among the cups.
5. Bake in the preheated oven for 20-25 minutes or until the muffins are set and the tops are golden brown.
6. Allow the muffins to cool for a few minutes in the tin before transferring them to a wire rack to cool completely.

Nutrition Information:
(Per serving - 1 muffin)
- Calories: 90, Total Fat: 5g, Saturated Fat: 2g, Cholesterol: 140mg, Sodium: 180mg, Total Carbohydrates: 4g, Dietary Fiber: 1g, Sugars: 2g, Protein: 8g
Note: Nutrition Information may vary based on specific ingredients and brands used.

22. Apple Cider Protein Pancakes

Start your day on a delicious and nutritious note with these Apple Cider Protein Pancakes. Packed with the wholesome goodness of apples and a protein boost, these pancakes are a perfect choice for a satisfying breakfast. Not only are they a treat for your taste buds, but they also align with the principles of Weight Watchers, making them an excellent option for those on a weight-conscious journey.

Serving: Makes 4 servings (2 pancakes per serving)
Preparation Time: 15 minutes
Ready Time: 25 minutes

Ingredients:
- 1 cup whole wheat flour
- 1 scoop vanilla protein powder
- 1 teaspoon baking powder
- 1/2 teaspoon ground cinnamon
- 1/4 teaspoon salt
- 1 cup unsweetened apple cider
- 1/4 cup unsweetened applesauce
- 1 large egg
- 1 tablespoon maple syrup
- 1 teaspoon vanilla extract
- Cooking spray for the pan

Instructions:
1. In a large mixing bowl, whisk together the whole wheat flour, protein powder, baking powder, cinnamon, and salt.
2. In a separate bowl, combine the apple cider, applesauce, egg, maple syrup, and vanilla extract. Mix well.
3. Add the wet ingredients to the dry ingredients, stirring until just combined. Be careful not to overmix; a few lumps are okay.
4. Heat a non-stick skillet or griddle over medium heat and lightly coat with cooking spray.
5. Pour 1/4 cup of batter onto the skillet for each pancake. Cook until bubbles form on the surface, then flip and cook the other side until golden brown.
6. Repeat until all the batter is used.
7. Serve the pancakes warm, topped with fresh apple slices or a drizzle of additional maple syrup if desired.

Nutrition Information
(per serving):

- Calories: 220, Protein: 12g, Carbohydrates: 38g, Dietary Fiber: 5g, Sugars: 10g, Fat: 3g, Saturated Fat: 1g, Cholesterol: 45mg, Sodium: 310mg
- Vitamin D: 1mcg
- Calcium: 120mg
- Iron: 2mg
- Potassium: 250mg

These Apple Cider Protein Pancakes offer a delightful blend of flavors and textures while keeping your breakfast both wholesome and satisfying. Enjoy guilt-free mornings with a plateful of these delicious pancakes!

23. Quinoa and Black Bean Breakfast Bowl

Start your day with a delicious and nutritious Quinoa and Black Bean Breakfast Bowl, a perfect addition to your Popular Weight Watchers Breakfast Recipes. Packed with protein, fiber, and flavor, this hearty breakfast bowl will keep you satisfied and energized throughout the morning. It's a delightful combination of quinoa, black beans, and fresh vegetables that will make your breakfast both enjoyable and healthy.

Serving: Serves 2
Preparation Time: 15 minutes
Ready Time: 25 minutes

Ingredients:
- 1 cup quinoa, rinsed
- 2 cups water
- 1 can (15 oz) black beans, drained and rinsed
- 1 cup cherry tomatoes, halved
- 1/2 cucumber, diced
- 1/4 cup red onion, finely chopped
- 1/4 cup fresh cilantro, chopped
- 1 avocado, sliced
- 2 tablespoons olive oil
- 1 tablespoon lime juice
- 1 teaspoon ground cumin
- Salt and pepper to taste

- Optional toppings: poached eggs, hot sauce

Instructions:
1. In a medium saucepan, combine the quinoa and water. Bring to a boil, then reduce heat to low, cover, and simmer for 15 minutes or until the quinoa is cooked and water is absorbed.
2. While the quinoa is cooking, prepare the black beans by heating them in a small saucepan over medium heat. Add cumin, salt, and pepper to taste. Stir well and cook until heated through.
3. In a large mixing bowl, combine the cooked quinoa, black beans, cherry tomatoes, cucumber, red onion, and cilantro.
4. In a small bowl, whisk together the olive oil and lime juice. Pour the dressing over the quinoa mixture and toss until well combined.
5. Divide the mixture into two bowls. Top each bowl with sliced avocado and any optional toppings you prefer, such as poached eggs or hot sauce.
6. Serve immediately and enjoy your wholesome Quinoa and Black Bean Breakfast Bowl!

Nutrition Information:
(Per serving)
- Calories: 450, Protein: 15g, Fat: 20g, Carbohydrates: 55g, Fiber: 12g, Sugar: 4g, Sodium: 350mg

Note: Nutrition Information is approximate and may vary based on specific ingredients used. Adjust quantities to meet your dietary preferences and needs.

24. Greek Yogurt and Honey Waffles

Start your day on a delightful and healthy note with these Greek Yogurt and Honey Waffles. Packed with protein-rich Greek yogurt and the natural sweetness of honey, these waffles are not only a delicious treat but also a perfect addition to your weight watchers' breakfast repertoire. Indulge guilt-free in the crispy exterior and fluffy interior of these waffles that will leave you satisfied and energized for the day ahead.

Serving: Makes 4 servings (2 waffles per serving)
Preparation Time: 15 minutes
Ready Time: 25 minutes

Ingredients:
- 1 cup whole wheat flour
- 1/2 cup rolled oats
- 1 tablespoon baking powder
- 1/2 teaspoon salt
- 1 cup non-fat Greek yogurt
- 1/2 cup skim milk
- 2 large eggs
- 2 tablespoons honey
- 1 teaspoon vanilla extract
- Cooking spray (for waffle iron)

Instructions:
1. Preheat your waffle iron according to the manufacturer's instructions.
2. In a large mixing bowl, combine the whole wheat flour, rolled oats, baking powder, and salt.
3. In a separate bowl, whisk together the Greek yogurt, skim milk, eggs, honey, and vanilla extract until well combined.
4. Pour the wet ingredients into the dry ingredients and stir until just combined. Be careful not to overmix; a few lumps are okay.
5. Lightly coat the waffle iron with cooking spray.
6. Spoon the batter onto the preheated waffle iron, spreading it evenly to cover the surface. Close the lid and cook until the waffles are golden brown and crisp.
7. Carefully remove the waffles and repeat the process until all the batter is used.
8. Serve the waffles warm, drizzled with an extra touch of honey if desired.

Nutrition Information
(per serving):
- Calories: 280, Protein: 17g, Carbohydrates: 45g, Fiber: 6g, Sugars: 10g, Fat: 4g, Saturated Fat: 1g, Cholesterol: 95mg, Sodium: 550mg
Note: Nutrition Information is approximate and may vary based on specific ingredients used.

25. Green Breakfast Smoothie

Start your day on a healthy note with this refreshing Green Breakfast Smoothie, a perfect addition to our collection of Popular Weight Watchers Breakfast Recipes. Packed with nutritious ingredients, this smoothie not only satisfies your taste buds but also supports your wellness journey. It's a delicious and low-point option that will keep you energized throughout the morning.

Serving: 2 servings
Preparation Time: 10 minutes
Ready Time: 10 minutes

Ingredients:
- 1 cup fresh spinach leaves, washed
- 1/2 cucumber, peeled and sliced
- 1/2 green apple, cored and chopped
- 1/2 ripe banana
- 1/2 cup non-fat Greek yogurt
- 1 tablespoon chia seeds
- 1 tablespoon honey (optional, for added sweetness)
- 1 cup unsweetened almond milk
- Ice cubes (optional)

Instructions:
1. In a blender, combine the fresh spinach leaves, cucumber slices, chopped green apple, ripe banana, non-fat Greek yogurt, chia seeds, and honey (if using).
2. Pour in the unsweetened almond milk to the blender.
3. If you prefer a colder smoothie, add a handful of ice cubes.
4. Blend on high speed until the mixture is smooth and creamy.
5. Stop the blender and scrape down the sides if needed, ensuring all ingredients are well combined.
6. Pour the green smoothie into glasses and serve immediately.
7. Garnish with a slice of cucumber or a sprinkle of chia seeds if desired.

Nutrition Information:
Per Serving

- Calories: 150, Total Fat: 3g, Saturated Fat: 0.5g, Cholesterol: 0mg, Sodium: 80mg, Total Carbohydrates: 27g, Dietary Fiber: 5g, Sugars: 15g, Protein: 7g

Note: Nutrition Information is approximate and may vary based on specific ingredients and brands used. Adjust the honey and yogurt quantities according to your taste preferences and Weight Watchers plan.

26. Spinach and Cheese Breakfast Quesadilla

Start your day on a healthy and delicious note with our Spinach and Cheese Breakfast Quesadilla. Packed with wholesome ingredients and bursting with flavor, this breakfast option is not only satisfying but also friendly to your Weight Watchers journey. The combination of spinach and cheese adds a nutritious punch, making it a perfect choice for those looking to enjoy a flavorful breakfast without compromising on their wellness goals.

Serving: Makes 2 quesadillas
Preparation Time: 10 minutes
Ready Time: 15 minutes

Ingredients:
- 4 whole wheat tortillas (8-inch diameter)
- 1 cup fresh spinach, chopped
- 1 cup reduced-fat shredded cheddar cheese
- 4 large eggs, beaten
- 1/2 cup diced tomatoes
- 1/4 cup diced red onion
- 1/4 cup diced bell peppers (any color)
- 1/2 teaspoon olive oil
- Salt and pepper to taste
- Optional toppings: salsa, Greek yogurt, or hot sauce

Instructions:
1. In a non-stick skillet, heat olive oil over medium heat. Add diced red onion and bell peppers, sautéing until softened.
2. Add chopped spinach to the skillet and cook until wilted. Season with salt and pepper to taste.

3. Push the vegetables to one side of the skillet and pour beaten eggs into the empty side. Scramble the eggs until fully cooked.
4. Remove the skillet from heat and mix the scrambled eggs with the sautéed vegetables.
5. On a separate griddle or skillet, place one whole wheat tortilla. Sprinkle half of the shredded cheddar cheese evenly over the tortilla.
6. Spoon half of the egg and vegetable mixture over the cheese, spreading it evenly.
7. Place a second tortilla on top, pressing down gently. Cook until the bottom tortilla is golden brown, then carefully flip the quesadilla and cook the other side until it's crispy and the cheese is melted.
8. Repeat the process for the second quesadilla.
9. Once both quesadillas are cooked, remove them from the griddle and let them cool for a minute before slicing into wedges.
10. Serve hot with diced tomatoes and your choice of optional toppings like salsa, Greek yogurt, or hot sauce.

Nutrition Information:
Per serving (1 quesadilla):
- Calories: 320, Total Fat: 16g, Saturated Fat: 6g, Cholesterol: 370mg, Sodium: 550mg, Total Carbohydrates: 26g, Dietary Fiber: 6g, Sugars: 2g, Protein: 20g

Enjoy this Spinach and Cheese Breakfast Quesadilla guilt-free as you embark on your Weight Watchers journey!

27. Baked Egg in Avocado

Start your day on a delicious and nutritious note with our Baked Egg in Avocado recipe—a perfect addition to your collection of Popular Weight Watchers Breakfast Recipes. Packed with protein, healthy fats, and a burst of flavor, this dish will keep you satisfied and energized throughout the morning. Indulge in a delightful combination of creamy avocado and perfectly baked eggs, creating a breakfast treat that's as wholesome as it is delicious.

Serving: 2 servings
Preparation Time: 10 minutes
Ready Time: 20 minutes

Ingredients:
- 2 ripe avocados
- 4 large eggs
- Salt and pepper, to taste
- Optional toppings: diced tomatoes, chopped cilantro, hot sauce

Instructions:
1. Preheat your oven to 425°F (220°C).
2. Cut the avocados in half and carefully scoop out a small portion of the flesh to create a well for the egg.
3. Place the avocado halves in a baking dish to prevent them from tipping over.
4. Crack one egg into each avocado half, ensuring not to overflow.
5. Season with salt and pepper to taste.
6. Bake in the preheated oven for approximately 15-20 minutes or until the eggs reach your desired level of doneness.
7. Remove from the oven and let them cool for a few minutes.
8. Sprinkle with optional toppings such as diced tomatoes, chopped cilantro, or a drizzle of hot sauce for an extra kick.
9. Serve immediately and enjoy the creamy goodness of Baked Egg in Avocado.

Nutrition Information:
Per serving (2 halves with eggs):
- Calories: 320, Protein: 12g, Fat: 26g, Carbohydrates: 12g, Fiber: 9g
Note: Nutrition Information may vary based on the size of avocados and specific toppings used.

28. Almond Joy Protein Shake

Start your day with a delicious and nutritious Almond Joy Protein Shake—a delightful blend of flavors reminiscent of the classic candy bar. Packed with the goodness of almonds, coconut, and chocolate, this protein shake is not only a tasty treat but also a fantastic way to kickstart your morning. Plus, it's a perfect addition to your Popular Weight Watchers Breakfast Recipes collection, helping you stay on track with your health and wellness goals.

Serving: 1 serving
Preparation Time: 5 minutes
Ready Time: 5 minutes

Ingredients:
- 1 cup unsweetened almond milk
- 1 scoop chocolate protein powder (ensure it fits your Weight Watchers plan)
- 2 tablespoons unsweetened shredded coconut
- 1 tablespoon almond butter
- 1/2 teaspoon almond extract
- 1/2 teaspoon coconut extract
- 1/2 teaspoon vanilla extract
- Ice cubes (optional)
- Sweetener of choice (optional, based on personal preference and Weight Watchers plan)

Instructions:
1. In a blender, combine the unsweetened almond milk, chocolate protein powder, unsweetened shredded coconut, almond butter, almond extract, coconut extract, and vanilla extract.
2. If you prefer a colder shake, add a handful of ice cubes to the blender.
3. Blend all the ingredients until smooth and creamy.
4. Taste the shake and add sweetener if desired, adjusting according to your personal preference and adherence to your Weight Watchers plan.
5. Pour the Almond Joy Protein Shake into a glass.
6. Garnish with a sprinkle of shredded coconut on top for an extra touch of flavor.
7. Enjoy your guilt-free and satisfying breakfast treat!

Nutrition Information:
Note: Nutritional values may vary based on specific ingredients used and individual preferences.
- Calories: Approximately 250 kcal, Protein: 25g, Fat: 15g, Carbohydrates: 8g, Fiber: 4g, Sugar: 1g
- Weight Watchers Points: X points (adjust based on your specific plan)

29. Peanut Butter and Jelly Overnight Oats

Jumpstart your day with a delicious and nutritious breakfast that's both satisfying and Weight Watchers-friendly. Our Peanut Butter and Jelly Overnight Oats are a delightful twist on a classic favorite. Packed with wholesome ingredients and the irresistible combination of peanut butter and jelly, this recipe will keep you energized and on track with your wellness goals. Make mornings easier with this simple, make-ahead meal that's as convenient as it is tasty.

Serving: 1 serving
Preparation Time: 10 minutes
Ready Time: Overnight (at least 6-8 hours of refrigeration)

Ingredients:
- 1/2 cup old-fashioned rolled oats
- 1/2 cup unsweetened almond milk (or your preferred milk)
- 1 tablespoon chia seeds
- 1 tablespoon powdered peanut butter
- 1/2 teaspoon vanilla extract
- 1 tablespoon sugar-free raspberry jam (or your favorite flavor)
- 1 tablespoon natural peanut butter
- Fresh berries for topping (optional)

Instructions:
1. In a mason jar or airtight container, combine the rolled oats, almond milk, chia seeds, powdered peanut butter, and vanilla extract. Mix well to ensure the ingredients are evenly distributed.
2. Spoon the sugar-free raspberry jam onto the oat mixture, and then add the natural peanut butter.
3. Stir gently to swirl the peanut butter and jelly into the oats without fully combining. This will create a delightful marbled effect.
4. Seal the jar or container and refrigerate overnight, or for at least 6-8 hours. This allows the oats to absorb the liquid and develop a creamy, pudding-like consistency.
5. Before serving, give the oats a good stir to combine all the flavors. If desired, top with fresh berries for an extra burst of sweetness and antioxidants.
6. Enjoy your Peanut Butter and Jelly Overnight Oats straight from the fridge or let them come to room temperature. Feel free to adjust the sweetness by adding more jam or peanut butter to suit your taste.

Nutrition Information:
- Calories: 350, Protein: 12g, Fat: 16g, Carbohydrates: 42g, Fiber: 10g, Sugar: 5g
- Weight Watchers SmartPoints: 8

Start your day right with this delightful Peanut Butter and Jelly Overnight Oats recipe that not only satisfies your cravings but also aligns with your wellness journey.

30. Breakfast Quiche with Spinach and Tomatoes

Start your day on a healthy and delicious note with our Breakfast Quiche featuring nutrient-rich spinach and vibrant tomatoes. This recipe is a perfect addition to your Weight Watchers journey, providing a satisfying and flavorful breakfast that won't compromise your wellness goals. Packed with protein and veggies, this quiche is a delightful way to kickstart your morning while staying on track with your Weight Watchers plan.

Serving: 4 servings
Preparation Time: 15 minutes
Ready Time: 45 minutes

Ingredients:
- 1 pre-made whole wheat pie crust
- 1 cup fresh spinach, chopped
- 1 cup cherry tomatoes, halved
- 1/2 cup red onion, finely chopped
- 1 cup reduced-fat shredded mozzarella cheese
- 4 large eggs
- 1 cup fat-free milk
- 1/2 teaspoon garlic powder
- 1/2 teaspoon onion powder
- Salt and pepper to taste

Instructions:
1. Preheat the oven to 375°F (190°C).

2. In a skillet over medium heat, sauté the chopped spinach, cherry tomatoes, and red onion until the vegetables are tender. Set aside to cool.
3. Roll out the whole wheat pie crust and press it into a pie dish, trimming any excess crust.
4. In a bowl, whisk together the eggs, fat-free milk, garlic powder, onion powder, salt, and pepper.
5. Spread the sautéed vegetables evenly over the pie crust. Sprinkle the shredded mozzarella cheese on top.
6. Pour the egg mixture over the vegetables and cheese.
7. Bake in the preheated oven for 30-35 minutes or until the quiche is set and the top is golden brown.
8. Allow the quiche to cool for a few minutes before slicing.

Nutrition Information
(per serving):
- Calories: 250, Total Fat: 12g, Saturated Fat: 4g, Cholesterol: 190mg, Sodium: 350mg, Total Carbohydrates: 20g, Dietary Fiber: 2g, Sugars: 2g, Protein: 15g

Note: Nutrition Information is approximate and may vary based on specific ingredients used. Adjust serving sizes accordingly to fit your Weight Watchers plan.

31. Banana Nut Overnight Oats

'Start your day right with a delicious and nutritious breakfast that will keep you energized and satisfied. These Banana Nut Overnight Oats are a perfect blend of flavors and a fantastic option for those following the Weight Watchers program. Packed with fiber, protein, and wholesome ingredients, this recipe is an excellent way to kickstart your morning routine."

Serving: 1
Preparation time: 10 minutes
Ready time: Overnight (at least 6-8 hours of refrigeration)

Ingredients:
- 1/2 cup rolled oats
- 1/2 cup unsweetened almond milk (or any milk of your choice)
- 1/2 medium ripe banana, mashed

- 1 tablespoon chopped walnuts
- 1 tablespoon honey or maple syrup (optional for added sweetness)
- 1/4 teaspoon vanilla extract
- Pinch of cinnamon (optional)
- Fresh banana slices and additional chopped walnuts for topping (optional)

Instructions:
1. In a mason jar or a container with a lid, combine the rolled oats, almond milk, mashed banana, chopped walnuts, honey or maple syrup (if using), vanilla extract, and a pinch of cinnamon if desired.
2. Stir the ingredients until well combined, ensuring that the oats are fully immersed in the liquid.
3. Seal the jar or container and refrigerate it overnight or for at least 6-8 hours to allow the oats to soften and absorb the flavors.
4. The next morning, give the oats a good stir. If the mixture is too thick, you can add a splash more almond milk to reach your desired consistency.
5. Top the oats with fresh banana slices and additional chopped walnuts for added texture and flavor, if desired, before serving.

Nutrition Information: (approximate values per serving)
- Calories: 350, Protein: 9g, Fat: 11g, Carbohydrates: 56g, Fiber: 7g, Sugar: 18g, Sodium: 90mg
Note: Nutrition Information may vary based on specific brands and quantities of ingredients used.
Enjoy your nutritious and delicious Banana Nut Overnight Oats as a wonderful way to start your day on the right track!

32. Veggie Frittata with Goat Cheese

Indulge in a delightful morning treat with this Veggie Frittata with Goat Cheese, a savory marvel perfect for a nourishing Weight Watchers breakfast. Packed with wholesome vegetables and the creamy tang of goat cheese, this frittata promises a burst of flavors that make healthy eating a pleasure.
Serving: 4 servings
Preparation time: 15 minutes

Ready time: 35 minutes

Ingredients:
- 6 large eggs
- 1/4 cup skim milk
- 1/2 cup diced bell peppers (any color)
- 1/2 cup chopped spinach
- 1/4 cup diced red onion
- 2 cloves garlic, minced
- 1/4 cup crumbled goat cheese
- Salt and pepper to taste
- Cooking spray or olive oil

Instructions:
1. Preheat your oven to 350°F (175°C).
2. In a mixing bowl, whisk together the eggs and skim milk until well combined. Season with salt and pepper to taste.
3. Heat an oven-safe skillet over medium heat and coat it with cooking spray or a small amount of olive oil.
4. Sauté the diced bell peppers, chopped spinach, red onion, and minced garlic until the vegetables are tender, for about 3-4 minutes.
5. Pour the egg mixture evenly over the sautéed vegetables in the skillet.
6. Sprinkle crumbled goat cheese evenly over the top of the frittata.
7. Allow the frittata to cook on the stovetop for 2-3 minutes or until the edges begin to set.
8. Transfer the skillet to the preheated oven and bake for 15-20 minutes or until the frittata is set in the center.
9. Once done, remove from the oven and let it cool slightly before slicing.
10. Serve warm, garnished with fresh herbs if desired.

Nutrition Information
(per serving):
- Calories: 160, Total Fat: 9g, Saturated Fat: 4g, Cholesterol: 280mg, Sodium: 230mg, Total Carbohydrates: 5g, Dietary Fiber: 1g, Sugars: 3g, Protein: 13g

Enjoy this delicious Veggie Frittata with Goat Cheese as a fantastic addition to your Weight Watchers breakfast repertoire—nutritious, flavorful, and satisfyingly light!

33. Blueberry Protein Pancakes

Start your morning right with these delicious Blueberry Protein Pancakes! Packed with wholesome ingredients and a boost of protein, they're a satisfying and nutritious way to kickstart your day. Plus, they fit perfectly into your Weight Watchers plan, making breakfast a delightful part of your journey to wellness.

Serving:
Makes 4 servings (2 pancakes per serving)
Preparation time:
15 minutes
Ready time:
25 minutes

Ingredients:
- 1 cup whole wheat flour
- 1 scoop vanilla protein powder
- 1 tablespoon baking powder
- 1/4 teaspoon salt
- 1 cup unsweetened almond milk (or any milk of choice)
- 1/4 cup plain Greek yogurt
- 1 egg
- 1 tablespoon honey or maple syrup
- 1 teaspoon vanilla extract
- 1 cup fresh blueberries

Instructions:
1. In a large mixing bowl, whisk together the whole wheat flour, protein powder, baking powder, and salt.
2. In another bowl, combine the almond milk, Greek yogurt, egg, honey or maple syrup, and vanilla extract. Mix until well combined.
3. Gently fold the wet ingredients into the dry ingredients until just combined. Be careful not to overmix; a few lumps are okay.
4. Gently fold in the fresh blueberries into the batter.
5. Heat a non-stick skillet or griddle over medium heat and lightly grease with cooking spray or a bit of oil.

6. Pour 1/4 cup of batter onto the skillet for each pancake. Cook until bubbles form on the surface, then flip and cook until golden brown on both sides, about 2-3 minutes per side.
7. Transfer the cooked pancakes to a plate and repeat with the remaining batter.
8. Serve warm with additional fresh blueberries, a drizzle of honey or maple syrup, and a dollop of Greek yogurt if desired.

Nutrition Information
(per serving):
- Calories: 230, Total Fat: 3g, Saturated Fat: 0.5g, Cholesterol: 40mg, Sodium: 480mg
- Total Carbohydrate: 40g, Dietary Fiber: 6g, Sugars: 9g, Protein: 14g
Enjoy these delightful pancakes guilt-free as part of your balanced breakfast routine!

34. Breakfast Burrito Bowl

Start your day on a delicious and nutritious note with this flavorful Breakfast Burrito Bowl. Packed with wholesome ingredients and designed with Weight Watchers in mind, this breakfast bowl is a perfect way to kickstart your morning. With a balance of protein, fiber, and healthy fats, it's a satisfying and guilt-free way to fuel your day.

Serving: 4 servings
Preparation Time: 15 minutes
Ready Time: 20 minutes

Ingredients:
- 1 cup quinoa, rinsed and cooked
- 4 large eggs
- 1 cup black beans, canned and drained
- 1 cup cherry tomatoes, halved
- 1 avocado, diced
- 1/2 cup red onion, finely chopped
- 1/4 cup fresh cilantro, chopped
- 1/2 cup salsa

- 1 tablespoon olive oil
- 1 teaspoon ground cumin
- 1 teaspoon chili powder
- Salt and pepper to taste
- Optional toppings: shredded cheese, Greek yogurt, lime wedges

Instructions:
1. Cook Quinoa: In a medium saucepan, combine 1 cup of rinsed quinoa with 2 cups of water. Bring to a boil, then reduce heat, cover, and simmer for 15 minutes or until quinoa is cooked and water is absorbed.
2. Prepare Eggs: In a non-stick skillet, heat olive oil over medium heat. Crack eggs into the skillet and cook to your liking (scrambled or fried).
3. Assemble Bowl: Divide the cooked quinoa among four bowls. Top each with black beans, cherry tomatoes, diced avocado, red onion, and cilantro.
4. Season: Sprinkle ground cumin, chili powder, salt, and pepper evenly over each bowl.
5. Add Eggs: Place the cooked eggs on top of each bowl.
6. Finish with Salsa: Drizzle salsa over the bowls for an extra burst of flavor.
7. Optional Toppings: Customize your bowl with optional toppings such as shredded cheese, a dollop of Greek yogurt, or a squeeze of fresh lime juice.
8. Serve: Enjoy your Breakfast Burrito Bowl immediately, savoring the combination of textures and flavors.

Nutrition Information
(per serving):
- Calories: 380, Protein: 17g, Carbohydrates: 40g, Dietary Fiber: 10g, Sugars: 3g, Fat: 18g, Saturated Fat: 3g, Cholesterol: 190mg, Sodium: 480mg

Note: Nutrition Information is approximate and may vary based on specific ingredients and portion sizes. Adjust quantities as needed to meet your dietary preferences and needs.

35. Egg White and Turkey Bacon Breakfast Sandwich

Start your day on a delicious and healthy note with our Egg White and Turkey Bacon Breakfast Sandwich—a perfect addition to your Weight Watchers journey. Packed with protein and flavor, this satisfying breakfast option will keep you energized throughout the morning. Say goodbye to the guilt and hello to a wholesome and tasty way to kickstart your day!

Serving: Serves 2
Preparation Time: 10 minutes
Ready Time: 15 minutes

Ingredients:
- 4 large egg whites
- 4 slices whole-grain English muffins, split and toasted
- 4 slices lean turkey bacon
- 2 slices reduced-fat Swiss cheese
- 1 medium tomato, sliced
- 1 cup fresh spinach leaves
- Salt and pepper to taste
- Cooking spray

Instructions:
1. Cook Turkey Bacon:
- Heat a non-stick skillet over medium heat and lightly coat it with cooking spray.
- Cook the turkey bacon slices until they are crispy and browned on both sides, usually about 2-3 minutes per side. Set aside.
2. Prepare Egg Whites:
- In a bowl, whisk the egg whites until they are well combined. Season with salt and pepper to taste.
- Pour the whisked egg whites into the skillet over medium heat, creating two round shapes.
- Allow the egg whites to cook undisturbed for 2-3 minutes or until the edges are set. Gently flip and cook for an additional 1-2 minutes.
3. Assemble the Sandwich:
- Place a slice of Swiss cheese on the bottom half of each toasted English muffin.
- Top the cheese with the cooked egg white rounds.
- Layer each sandwich with 2 slices of turkey bacon, tomato slices, and fresh spinach leaves.

- Complete the sandwich with the top half of the English muffin.
4. Serve:
- Slice each sandwich in half and serve immediately.

Nutrition Information:
(Per Serving)
- Calories: 280, Protein: 22g, Carbohydrates: 26g, Dietary Fiber: 5g, Sugars: 4g, Total Fat: 10g, Saturated Fat: 3.5g, Cholesterol: 30mg, Sodium: 650mg
Note: Nutrition Information is approximate and may vary based on specific ingredients used. Adjust serving sizes to meet your dietary preferences and Weight Watchers plan.

36. Raspberry Chia Pudding

Indulge in a guilt-free and nutritious start to your day with our delectable Raspberry Chia Pudding, specially crafted for those following the Weight Watchers program. This vibrant and satisfying breakfast is not only a treat for your taste buds but also a wholesome choice to keep you energized throughout the morning. Packed with the goodness of chia seeds and the delightful sweetness of raspberries, this recipe is a perfect blend of flavor and wellness.

Serving: Makes 4 servings
Preparation Time: 15 minutes
Ready Time: 4 hours (including chilling time)

Ingredients:
- 1 cup fresh raspberries
- 1/4 cup maple syrup (adjust to taste)
- 1 teaspoon vanilla extract
- 1/2 cup chia seeds
- 2 cups unsweetened almond milk (or any milk of your choice)
- Optional toppings: additional raspberries, sliced almonds, mint leaves

Instructions:
1. Prepare the Raspberry Puree:

- In a blender, combine fresh raspberries, maple syrup, and vanilla extract. Blend until smooth.
- Strain the raspberry puree through a fine mesh sieve to remove seeds. Set aside.

2. Mix Chia Seeds and Almond Milk:
- In a medium-sized bowl, whisk together chia seeds and almond milk until well combined.
- Let the mixture sit for 5-10 minutes, stirring occasionally to prevent clumping.

3. Combine Raspberry Puree with Chia Mixture:
- Gently fold the raspberry puree into the chia seed mixture until evenly distributed.
- Taste and adjust sweetness by adding more maple syrup if desired.

4. Refrigerate to Set:
- Divide the mixture into four serving jars or bowls.
- Cover and refrigerate for at least 4 hours or overnight until the pudding has a thick, pudding-like consistency.

5. Serve and Enjoy:
- Before serving, garnish with additional raspberries, sliced almonds, or mint leaves for an extra burst of freshness.

Nutrition Information
(per serving):
- Calories: 180, Total Fat: 8g, Saturated Fat: 1g, Trans Fat: 0g, Cholesterol: 0mg, Sodium: 70mg, Total Carbohydrates: 25g, Dietary Fiber: 10g, Sugars: 10g, Protein: 5g

Note: Nutrition Information may vary based on specific ingredients and brands used.

37. Greek Yogurt and Mixed Berry Parfait

Start your day on a healthy and delicious note with this Greek Yogurt and Mixed Berry Parfait – a perfect addition to your Weight Watchers breakfast repertoire. Packed with protein, vitamins, and antioxidants, this delightful parfait not only satisfies your taste buds but also helps you stay on track with your weight management goals.

Serving: 2 servings

Preparation Time: 10 minutes
Ready Time: 10 minutes

Ingredients:
- 2 cups non-fat Greek yogurt
- 1 cup mixed berries (strawberries, blueberries, raspberries)
- 2 tablespoons honey or maple syrup (optional)
- 1/2 cup granola (choose a low-sugar or sugar-free option for a healthier choice)
- 1 teaspoon chia seeds (optional)
- Fresh mint leaves for garnish (optional)

Instructions:
1. Prepare the Berries:
Wash and dice the strawberries, and mix them with blueberries and raspberries in a bowl. Toss gently to combine.
2. Layer the Parfait:
Take two serving glasses or bowls and begin layering. Start with a spoonful of Greek yogurt at the bottom of each glass.
3. Add Berries:
Top the yogurt with a layer of mixed berries, spreading them evenly.
4. Repeat Layers:
Repeat the process, adding another layer of Greek yogurt followed by berries until the glass is almost full.
5. Sweeten (Optional):
Drizzle honey or maple syrup over the top for a touch of sweetness, if desired.
6. Top with Granola:
Sprinkle granola evenly over the parfait, adding a satisfying crunch to each bite.
7. Enhance with Chia Seeds (Optional):
For added nutritional benefits, sprinkle chia seeds over the granola.
8. Garnish (Optional):
Garnish with fresh mint leaves for a burst of freshness.
9. Serve:
Serve immediately and enjoy the layers of creamy yogurt, juicy berries, and crunchy granola.

Nutrition Information
(per serving):

- Calories: 250, Protein: 20g, Carbohydrates: 40g, Dietary Fiber: 5g, Sugars: 20g, Fat: 2g, Saturated Fat: 0g, Cholesterol: 5mg, Sodium: 60mg
Note: Nutrition Information may vary based on specific brands and quantities of ingredients used. Adjustments can be made for personal dietary preferences and requirements.

38. Spinach and Mushroom Egg White Omelette

Start your day on a healthy note with this delightful Spinach and Mushroom Egg White Omelette—a perfect addition to your Weight Watchers breakfast repertoire. Packed with nutrient-rich egg whites, vibrant spinach, and savory mushrooms, this omelette is not only delicious but also a guilt-free way to fuel your morning. With a burst of flavors and minimal SmartPoints, it's an ideal choice for those looking to maintain a balanced and satisfying breakfast routine.

Serving: Makes 1 serving
Preparation Time: 10 minutes
Ready Time: 15 minutes

Ingredients:
- 1 cup egg whites
- 1/2 cup fresh spinach, chopped
- 1/4 cup mushrooms, sliced
- 1/4 cup onion, finely chopped
- 1 clove garlic, minced
- 1 tablespoon olive oil
- Salt and pepper to taste
- 1 tablespoon feta cheese, crumbled (optional, for garnish)
- Fresh herbs (such as parsley or chives), chopped, for garnish

Instructions:
1. Prepare the Vegetables: In a non-stick skillet, heat the olive oil over medium heat. Add the chopped onion and garlic, sautéing until softened and fragrant.
2. Add Mushrooms and Spinach: Toss in the sliced mushrooms and chopped spinach. Cook until the vegetables are tender and the spinach is wilted.

3. Whisk Egg Whites: In a bowl, whisk the egg whites until frothy. Season with salt and pepper to taste.
4. Combine and Cook: Pour the whisked egg whites over the sautéed vegetables in the skillet. Allow the eggs to set around the edges, and gently lift them with a spatula to let any uncooked egg flow underneath.
5. Fold and Finish: Once the eggs are mostly set, carefully fold the omelette in half. Continue cooking for another minute or until the omelette is cooked through but still moist.
6. Garnish and Serve: Slide the omelette onto a plate and sprinkle with crumbled feta cheese (if using) and fresh herbs for a burst of flavor.

Nutrition Information:
Note: Nutrition Information may vary based on specific ingredients and optional additions.
- Calories: ~200 kcal, Protein: ~25g, Carbohydrates: ~8g, Fat: ~8g, Fiber: ~2g, Sugar: ~3g
Feel free to adjust ingredients and portions according to your dietary preferences and Weight Watchers plan. Enjoy your wholesome and satisfying breakfast!

39. Whole Wheat Pancakes with Cinnamon Apples

Start your day on a delicious and nutritious note with our Whole Wheat Pancakes with Cinnamon Apples! This delightful breakfast option is not only a treat for your taste buds but also a smart choice for those on the Weight Watchers program. Packed with whole grains and topped with a spiced apple compote, these pancakes offer a satisfying and wholesome start to your morning.

Serving: Makes approximately 6 servings (2 pancakes per serving).
Preparation Time: 15 minutes
Ready Time: 25 minutes

Ingredients:
- 1 cup whole wheat flour
- 1 tablespoon sugar
- 1 teaspoon baking powder
- 1/2 teaspoon baking soda

- 1/4 teaspoon salt
- 1 cup low-fat buttermilk
- 1 large egg
- 2 tablespoons unsalted butter, melted
- 1 teaspoon vanilla extract

For the Cinnamon Apples:
- 2 medium apples, peeled, cored, and thinly sliced
- 1 tablespoon unsalted butter
- 2 tablespoons brown sugar
- 1/2 teaspoon ground cinnamon
- Pinch of nutmeg (optional)

Instructions:
1. In a large bowl, whisk together the whole wheat flour, sugar, baking powder, baking soda, and salt.
2. In a separate bowl, whisk together the buttermilk, egg, melted butter, and vanilla extract.
3. Pour the wet ingredients into the dry ingredients and gently stir until just combined. Be careful not to overmix; a few lumps are okay.
4. Heat a griddle or non-stick skillet over medium heat. Lightly coat with cooking spray.
5. Pour 1/4 cup of batter onto the griddle for each pancake. Cook until bubbles form on the surface, then flip and cook until golden brown on the other side. Repeat with the remaining batter.
6. While the pancakes are cooking, prepare the Cinnamon Apples. In a skillet over medium heat, melt the butter. Add the sliced apples, brown sugar, cinnamon, and nutmeg (if using). Cook until the apples are tender and coated in a sweet cinnamon glaze.
7. Serve the pancakes topped with a generous spoonful of the Cinnamon Apples.

Nutrition Information:
(Per serving, including Cinnamon Apples)
- Calories: 220, Total Fat: 7g, Saturated Fat: 4g, Cholesterol: 45mg, Sodium: 350mg, Total Carbohydrates: 37g, Dietary Fiber: 5g, Sugars: 15g, Protein: 5g

These Whole Wheat Pancakes with Cinnamon Apples are a delightful way to indulge in a comforting breakfast while keeping your wellness goals in check. Enjoy the perfect balance of flavors and textures to kickstart your day!

40. Breakfast Tacos with Salsa

Start your day on a delicious and healthy note with these Breakfast Tacos with Salsa—a perfect addition to your Weight Watchers journey. Packed with vibrant flavors and nutritious ingredients, these tacos are a delightful way to fuel your morning while keeping your wellness goals in check.

Serving: This recipe yields 4 servings.
Preparation Time: 15 minutes
Ready Time: 20 minutes

Ingredients:
- 8 small whole wheat or corn tortillas
- 8 large eggs
- 1 cup black beans, drained and rinsed
- 1 cup cherry tomatoes, diced
- 1/2 cup red onion, finely chopped
- 1/4 cup fresh cilantro, chopped
- 1 avocado, sliced
- 1 cup reduced-fat shredded cheddar cheese
- Salt and pepper to taste

Instructions:
1. In a non-stick skillet over medium heat, warm the tortillas for about 30 seconds on each side. Keep them warm in a kitchen towel.
2. In the same skillet, lightly spray with cooking spray and scramble the eggs until fully cooked. Season with salt and pepper to taste.
3. Assemble the tacos by placing a spoonful of scrambled eggs onto each tortilla.
4. Top with black beans, cherry tomatoes, red onion, cilantro, avocado slices, and a sprinkle of shredded cheddar cheese.
5. Fold the tacos in half and serve immediately.

Nutrition Information:
(Per serving)

- Calories: 320, Protein: 18g, Carbohydrates: 28g, Dietary Fiber: 8g, Sugars: 2g, Total Fat: 16g, Saturated Fat: 4g, Cholesterol: 380mg, Sodium: 340mg

These Breakfast Tacos with Salsa are not only a delicious way to kickstart your day but also a smart choice for those mindful of their weight. Enjoy a satisfying breakfast that aligns with your wellness goals!

41. Peanut Butter and Banana Protein Pancakes

Start your day with a delicious and nutritious twist on a classic breakfast favorite – Peanut Butter and Banana Protein Pancakes. Packed with wholesome ingredients and a protein punch, these pancakes are not only a treat for your taste buds but also a perfect choice for those following a Weight Watchers plan. The combination of creamy peanut butter and ripe bananas creates a delightful harmony of flavors that will leave you satisfied and energized for the day ahead.

Serving: Makes approximately 6 pancakes
Preparation Time: 15 minutes
Ready Time: 25 minutes

Ingredients:
- 1 cup whole wheat flour
- 1 scoop vanilla protein powder
- 1 teaspoon baking powder
- 1/2 teaspoon baking soda
- 1/4 teaspoon salt
- 1 cup unsweetened almond milk (or any preferred milk)
- 1 ripe banana, mashed
- 2 tablespoons natural peanut butter
- 1 large egg
- 1 teaspoon vanilla extract
- Cooking spray or a small amount of butter for greasing the pan

Instructions:
1. In a large mixing bowl, combine the whole wheat flour, protein powder, baking powder, baking soda, and salt. Mix well to ensure even distribution of dry ingredients.

2. In a separate bowl, whisk together the almond milk, mashed banana, peanut butter, egg, and vanilla extract until well combined.
3. Pour the wet ingredients into the dry ingredients and gently stir until just combined. Be careful not to overmix; a few lumps are okay.
4. Heat a non-stick skillet or griddle over medium heat and lightly coat with cooking spray or a small amount of butter.
5. Pour 1/4 cup of batter onto the hot skillet for each pancake. Cook until bubbles form on the surface, then flip and cook the other side until golden brown.
6. Repeat the process until all the batter is used.
7. Serve the pancakes warm, topped with additional sliced banana, a drizzle of peanut butter, or your favorite sugar-free syrup.

Nutrition Information:
(per serving, based on 1 pancake)
- Calories: 120, Protein: 7g, Fat: 4g, Carbohydrates: 16g, Fiber: 3g, Sugar: 2g, Sodium: 230mg

Enjoy these Peanut Butter and Banana Protein Pancakes guilt-free as you kickstart your day with a delicious and satisfying breakfast!

42. Breakfast Stuffed Sweet Potatoes

'Start your day with a delicious and nutritious twist on breakfast by indulging in these Breakfast Stuffed Sweet Potatoes. Packed with wholesome ingredients and bursting with flavor, this Weight Watchers-friendly recipe offers a perfect balance of taste and health. These stuffed sweet potatoes are a delightful and filling way to kickstart your morning routine."

Serving:
- Serves: 4

Preparation time:
- Prep: 10 minutes

Ready time:
- Ready in: 50 minutes

Ingredients:
- 4 medium-sized sweet potatoes
- 4 large eggs

- 1 cup baby spinach, chopped
- 1/2 cup cherry tomatoes, diced
- 1/4 cup red onion, finely chopped
- 1/4 cup reduced-fat shredded cheddar cheese
- Salt and pepper to taste
- Cooking spray or olive oil for baking

Instructions:
1. Preheat your oven to 400°F (200°C).
2. Wash the sweet potatoes thoroughly and pat them dry. Using a fork, prick the sweet potatoes a few times around each one.
3. Place the sweet potatoes on a baking sheet lined with parchment paper. Lightly coat them with cooking spray or rub a small amount of olive oil over the skins.
4. Bake the sweet potatoes in the preheated oven for 45-50 minutes, or until they are tender and easily pierced with a fork.
5. While the sweet potatoes are baking, prepare the filling. In a skillet over medium heat, lightly spray with cooking spray or add a small amount of olive oil. Sauté the red onion until it becomes translucent.
6. Add the chopped spinach and cherry tomatoes to the skillet. Cook for 2-3 minutes until the spinach wilts and the tomatoes soften slightly. Season with salt and pepper to taste.
7. Once the sweet potatoes are done, remove them from the oven and let them cool for a few minutes.
8. Carefully slice each sweet potato lengthwise, creating a pocket for the filling.
9. Evenly distribute the sautéed vegetable mixture among the sweet potatoes' pockets.
10. Crack an egg into each sweet potato pocket on top of the vegetable mixture.
11. Sprinkle the shredded cheddar cheese over each stuffed sweet potato.
12. Place the stuffed sweet potatoes back in the oven and bake for an additional 10-15 minutes, or until the egg whites are set and the cheese is melted and bubbly.
13. Remove from the oven and let them cool slightly before serving.

Nutrition Information
(per serving):

- Calories: Approximately 250, Total Fat: 7g, Saturated Fat: 3g, Cholesterol: 200mg, Sodium: 250mg, Total Carbohydrates: 35g, Dietary Fiber: 5g, Sugars: 10g, Protein: 11g
(

Nutrition Information is approximate and may vary based on specific ingredients used.)
Enjoy your delicious Breakfast Stuffed Sweet Potatoes, a fantastic way to energize your morning while staying on track with your Weight Watchers goals!

43. Strawberry Almond Oatmeal

Start your day with a burst of flavors and wholesome goodness with this delightful Strawberry Almond Oatmeal recipe. Combining the sweetness of fresh strawberries, the nuttiness of almonds, and the heartiness of oatmeal, this breakfast dish is both satisfying and healthy. Perfect for those following Weight Watchers, it's a nutritious and delicious way to kickstart your morning routine.

Serving: This recipe serves 2.
Preparation Time: 10 minutes
Ready Time: 15 minutes

Ingredients:
- 1 cup old-fashioned rolled oats
- 2 cups unsweetened almond milk
- 1 cup fresh strawberries, hulled and sliced
- 2 tablespoons sliced almonds
- 1 tablespoon honey or maple syrup (optional)
- 1/2 teaspoon vanilla extract
- Pinch of salt

Instructions:
1. In a saucepan, combine the almond milk, rolled oats, and a pinch of salt. Bring to a gentle boil over medium heat, stirring occasionally.

2. Reduce the heat to low and simmer the oats for about 5-7 minutes or until they reach your desired consistency, stirring occasionally to prevent sticking.
3. Remove the saucepan from heat and stir in the vanilla extract.
4. Divide the cooked oatmeal into serving bowls.
5. Top each bowl with sliced strawberries and sliced almonds.
6. If desired, drizzle a little honey or maple syrup over the oatmeal for added sweetness.
7. Serve warm and enjoy your delicious Strawberry Almond Oatmeal!

Nutrition Information
(per serving):
- Calories: 280, Total Fat: 9g, Saturated Fat: 1g, Trans Fat: 0g, Cholesterol: 0mg, Sodium: 160mg, Total Carbohydrates: 42g, Dietary Fiber: 7g, Sugars: 7g, Protein: 9g
- Vitamin D: 25IU
- Calcium: 350mg
- Iron: 3mg
- Potassium: 350mg
(Note: Nutrition Information is approximate and may vary based on specific ingredients used.)
Enjoy this nutritious and flavorful Strawberry Almond Oatmeal as a fulfilling breakfast option, perfect for anyone seeking a delicious Weight Watchers-friendly meal to start their day.

44. Egg White and Turkey Sausage Breakfast Wrap

This Egg White and Turkey Sausage Breakfast Wrap is a delectable way to start your day while staying mindful of your health goals. Packed with protein and bursting with flavor, this dish is perfect for those following the Weight Watchers program or anyone looking for a satisfying breakfast option that won't derail their wellness journey. It's a simple, wholesome, and delicious morning meal that keeps you fueled and ready to take on the day.
 Serving:
Serves: 2
 Preparation time:
Prep: 10 minutes

Ready time:
Ready in: 20 minutes

Ingredients:
- 4 large egg whites
- 4 whole wheat tortillas (8-inch size)
- 4 turkey sausage patties, cooked and crumbled
- 1/2 cup diced bell peppers (any color)
- 1/4 cup diced onions
- 1/2 cup reduced-fat shredded cheddar cheese
- Salt and pepper to taste
- Cooking spray or olive oil for sautéing

Instructions:
1. Prepare the Egg Whites: In a bowl, whisk the egg whites with a pinch of salt and pepper until frothy.
2. Sauté Vegetables: Heat a non-stick skillet over medium heat and lightly coat it with cooking spray or olive oil. Sauté the diced bell peppers and onions until they are softened, for about 3-4 minutes.
3. Cook the Egg Whites: Pour the whisked egg whites into the skillet with the sautéed vegetables. Cook, stirring occasionally, until the eggs are set and no longer runny, for about 3-4 minutes. Remove from heat.
4. Assemble the Wraps: Lay out the whole wheat tortillas and divide the cooked egg whites equally among them. Spread the egg whites evenly over each tortilla.
5. Add Turkey Sausage and Cheese: Distribute the crumbled turkey sausage and shredded cheddar cheese evenly over the egg whites on each tortilla.
6. Wrap it Up: Carefully fold in the sides of the tortilla, then roll it up tightly to form a wrap.
7. Heat the Wraps (Optional): If desired, return the assembled wraps to the skillet over medium heat and cook for 1-2 minutes on each side to lightly toast and melt the cheese.
8. Serve: Slice the wraps in half diagonally and serve warm.

Nutrition Information
(per serving):
- Calories: 290, Total Fat: 10g, Saturated Fat: 4g, Cholesterol: 60mg, Sodium: 720mg

- Total Carbohydrate: 26g, Dietary Fiber: 4g, Sugars: 3g, Protein: 24g
Note: Nutritional values are approximate and may vary depending on specific ingredients used. Adjustments can be made based on individual dietary needs or preferences.

45. Quinoa and Berry Breakfast Salad

Start your day on a healthy note with this delightful Quinoa and Berry Breakfast Salad, a perfect addition to our collection of Popular Weight Watchers Breakfast Recipes. Packed with the goodness of quinoa, fresh berries, and a light dressing, this salad not only satisfies your taste buds but also supports your weight management goals. Enjoy a nutritious and delicious breakfast that fuels your day with energy.

Serving: Serves 4
Preparation Time: 15 minutes
Ready Time: 30 minutes

Ingredients:
- 1 cup quinoa, rinsed
- 2 cups water
- 1 cup fresh strawberries, hulled and sliced
- 1 cup fresh blueberries
- 1 cup fresh raspberries
- 1/4 cup chopped fresh mint leaves
- 1/4 cup chopped walnuts (optional)

Dressing:
- 2 tablespoons fresh orange juice
- 1 tablespoon honey or maple syrup
- 1 teaspoon grated orange zest
- 1 tablespoon olive oil

Instructions:
1. Cook Quinoa:
- In a medium saucepan, combine quinoa and water.
- Bring to a boil, then reduce heat to low, cover, and simmer for 15 minutes or until quinoa is cooked and water is absorbed.
- Fluff quinoa with a fork and let it cool to room temperature.

2. Prepare Dressing:
- In a small bowl, whisk together orange juice, honey or maple syrup, orange zest, and olive oil until well combined. Set aside.
3. Assemble Salad:
- In a large mixing bowl, combine the cooked quinoa, strawberries, blueberries, raspberries, mint leaves, and walnuts (if using).
- Pour the dressing over the salad and gently toss until all ingredients are well coated.
4. Chill and Serve:
- Refrigerate the salad for at least 15 minutes to allow flavors to meld.
- Serve chilled, garnished with additional mint leaves if desired.

Nutrition Information:
(Per serving)
- Calories: 250, Total Fat: 7g, Saturated Fat: 1g, Trans Fat: 0g, Cholesterol: 0mg, Sodium: 5mg, Total Carbohydrates: 44g, Dietary Fiber: 6g, Sugars: 10g, Protein: 6g
Enjoy a guilt-free, delicious breakfast that will keep you energized and satisfied throughout the morning!

46. Cinnamon Raisin Protein French Toast

Start your day on a delicious and nutritious note with our Cinnamon Raisin Protein French Toast. This Weight Watchers-friendly breakfast is a perfect blend of warm, comforting flavors and a protein boost to keep you satisfied throughout the morning. With the sweet aroma of cinnamon, the plump juiciness of raisins, and the added protein kick, this recipe is a delightful twist on a classic breakfast favorite.

Serving: Serves 4
Preparation Time: 15 minutes
Ready Time: 20 minutes

Ingredients:
- 8 slices of whole wheat bread (preferably low-point bread for Weight Watchers)
- 4 large eggs
- 1 cup unsweetened almond milk (or any milk of your choice)

- 1 scoop vanilla protein powder
- 1 teaspoon ground cinnamon
- 1/2 teaspoon vanilla extract
- 1/4 cup raisins
- Cooking spray or a pat of butter for the pan

Instructions:
1. In a mixing bowl, whisk together the eggs, almond milk, vanilla protein powder, ground cinnamon, and vanilla extract until well combined.
2. Stir in the raisins, ensuring they are evenly distributed throughout the mixture.
3. Preheat a non-stick skillet or griddle over medium heat and lightly coat it with cooking spray or butter.
4. Dip each slice of bread into the egg mixture, ensuring both sides are well-coated. Allow any excess to drip off.
5. Place the coated bread slices on the preheated skillet and cook for 2-3 minutes per side or until golden brown and cooked through.
6. Repeat the process until all the bread slices are cooked, adding more cooking spray or butter as needed.
7. Serve the Cinnamon Raisin Protein French Toast warm, topped with fresh fruit, a drizzle of sugar-free syrup, or a dollop of Greek yogurt if desired.

Nutrition Information
(per serving):
- Calories: XXX, Total Fat: XXg, Saturated Fat: Xg, Cholesterol: XXXmg, Sodium: XXXmg, Total Carbohydrates: XXg, Dietary Fiber: Xg, Sugars: XXg, Protein: XXg
(Note: Nutrition Information may vary based on specific brands of ingredients used and portion sizes.)

47. Greek Yogurt and Granola Parfait

Start your day with a delightful and nutritious Greek Yogurt and Granola Parfait, a perfect addition to your Popular Weight Watchers Breakfast repertoire. This wholesome and satisfying parfait combines the creamy goodness of Greek yogurt with the crunch of granola and the sweetness of fresh fruits. Packed with protein and fiber, it's a smart and delicious way to kickstart your morning while keeping your weight management goals in check.

Serving: Serves 2
Preparation Time: 10 minutes
Ready Time: 10 minutes

Ingredients:
- 1 cup non-fat Greek yogurt
- 1/2 cup granola (choose a low-sugar or sugar-free option for a healthier choice)
- 1 cup mixed fresh berries (strawberries, blueberries, raspberries)
- 2 tablespoons honey or maple syrup (optional for added sweetness)
- 1/4 cup chopped nuts (almonds, walnuts, or your preferred choice)
- Fresh mint leaves for garnish (optional)

Instructions:
1. In two serving glasses or bowls, start by layering 1/4 cup of Greek yogurt at the bottom.
2. Add 2 tablespoons of granola on top of the yogurt layer.
3. Place a handful of mixed berries over the granola.
4. Repeat the layers until you reach the top of the glass or bowl, finishing with a layer of berries.
5. Drizzle honey or maple syrup over the top for added sweetness if desired.
6. Sprinkle chopped nuts on the top layer for a delightful crunch.
7. Garnish with fresh mint leaves for a burst of freshness (optional).
8. Serve immediately and enjoy your delicious and satisfying Greek Yogurt and Granola Parfait!

Nutrition Information:
Note: Nutrition Information may vary based on specific ingredients and brands used.
- Calories: Approximately 250 per serving, Protein: 15g, Fat: 8g, Carbohydrates: 30g, Fiber: 5g, Sugar: 15g (adjust based on the sweetness of the yogurt and granola used)
This delightful parfait is not only a treat for your taste buds but also a great way to stay on track with your weight management goals. Enjoy a

flavorful and filling breakfast that sets a positive tone for the rest of your day!

48. Spinach and Tomato Breakfast Quiche

Start your day with a delightful and nutritious Spinach and Tomato Breakfast Quiche, a perfect addition to your collection of Popular Weight Watchers Breakfast Recipes. Packed with the goodness of spinach, tomatoes, and a savory blend of ingredients, this quiche is a flavorful and satisfying way to kickstart your morning while staying mindful of your health and wellness goals.

Serving: 6 servings
Preparation Time: 15 minutes
Ready Time: 45 minutes

Ingredients:
- 1 pre-made whole wheat pie crust
- 1 cup fresh spinach, chopped
- 1 cup cherry tomatoes, halved
- 1/2 cup red bell pepper, diced
- 1/2 cup red onion, finely chopped
- 1 cup reduced-fat shredded cheddar cheese
- 4 large eggs
- 1 cup skim milk
- 1 teaspoon olive oil
- 1 teaspoon Dijon mustard
- 1/2 teaspoon salt
- 1/4 teaspoon black pepper
- 1/4 teaspoon paprika

Instructions:
1. Preheat the oven to 375°F (190°C).
2. In a skillet over medium heat, add olive oil. Sauté red bell pepper and red onion until softened, about 3-4 minutes.
3. In a bowl, whisk together eggs, milk, Dijon mustard, salt, black pepper, and paprika until well combined.

4. Place the whole wheat pie crust in a pie dish and spread the sautéed vegetables evenly over the crust.
5. Sprinkle chopped spinach, halved cherry tomatoes, and shredded cheddar cheese over the vegetables.
6. Pour the egg mixture over the vegetables and cheese.
7. Bake in the preheated oven for 30-35 minutes or until the center is set and the top is golden brown.
8. Allow the quiche to cool for a few minutes before slicing into wedges.
9. Serve warm and enjoy a delicious and satisfying Spinach and Tomato Breakfast Quiche.

Nutrition Information
(per serving):
- Calories: 240, Total Fat: 14g, Saturated Fat: 6g, Trans Fat: 0g, Cholesterol: 145mg, Sodium: 480mg, Total Carbohydrates: 17g, Dietary Fiber: 2g, Sugars: 3g, Protein: 12g
Note: Nutrition Information is approximate and may vary based on specific ingredients used. Adjustments can be made based on individual dietary needs and preferences.

49. Veggie Breakfast Skillet

Start your day on a healthy and satisfying note with our Veggie Breakfast Skillet—a delightful blend of colorful vegetables and savory flavors that will kickstart your morning with a burst of energy. Packed with nutrient-rich ingredients, this recipe is not only delicious but also a perfect addition to your weight watchers' breakfast repertoire.

Serving: Serves 4
Preparation Time: 15 minutes
Ready Time: 25 minutes

Ingredients:
- 1 tablespoon olive oil
- 1 red bell pepper, diced
- 1 yellow bell pepper, diced
- 1 small red onion, finely chopped
- 2 cloves garlic, minced

- 2 medium zucchinis, diced
- 1 cup cherry tomatoes, halved
- 4 cups fresh spinach leaves
- 8 large eggs
- Salt and pepper to taste
- 1 teaspoon paprika
- 1/2 teaspoon cumin
- Fresh parsley, chopped (for garnish)

Instructions:
1. Heat olive oil in a large skillet over medium heat.
2. Add diced red and yellow bell peppers, and sauté until they begin to soften, approximately 3-4 minutes.
3. Add finely chopped red onion and minced garlic to the skillet, stirring until the onions become translucent, about 2 minutes.
4. Toss in diced zucchinis and cherry tomatoes, continuing to cook until the vegetables are tender, about 5 minutes.
5. Add fresh spinach leaves to the skillet, stirring until they wilt and become incorporated with the other vegetables.
6. Create small wells in the vegetable mixture and crack one egg into each well.
7. Season the eggs and vegetables with salt, pepper, paprika, and cumin to taste.
8. Cover the skillet and cook until the egg whites are set, and the yolks are cooked to your preference, approximately 5-7 minutes.
9. Garnish with fresh chopped parsley and serve hot.

Nutrition Information:
(Per Serving)
- Calories: 220, Protein: 15g, Carbohydrates: 12g, Dietary Fiber: 4g, Sugars: 6g, Total Fat: 14g, Saturated Fat: 3.5g, Cholesterol: 370mg, Sodium: 280mg
- Vitamin D: 20%
- Calcium: 10%
- Iron: 15%

This Veggie Breakfast Skillet is a delicious and nutritious way to start your day, offering a hearty breakfast option that aligns with your weight watchers' goals. Enjoy the flavors and fuel your morning with wholesome goodness!

50. Pumpkin Pie Protein Smoothie

Start your day on a nutritious and delicious note with our Pumpkin Pie Protein Smoothie—a perfect addition to your Weight Watchers breakfast routine. Packed with the goodness of pumpkin and enriched with protein, this smoothie will keep you satisfied and energized throughout the morning. With the warm flavors of pumpkin pie, it's a guilt-free treat that will make your breakfast both enjoyable and nutritious.

Serving: 2 servings
Preparation Time: 10 minutes
Ready Time: 10 minutes

Ingredients:
- 1 cup canned pumpkin puree
- 1 cup unsweetened almond milk
- 2 scoops vanilla protein powder
- 1 banana, frozen
- 1/2 teaspoon ground cinnamon
- 1/4 teaspoon ground nutmeg
- 1/4 teaspoon ground ginger
- 1 tablespoon chia seeds
- 1 tablespoon honey or maple syrup (optional, based on sweetness preference)
- Ice cubes (optional)

Instructions:
1. In a blender, combine the canned pumpkin puree, unsweetened almond milk, vanilla protein powder, frozen banana, ground cinnamon, ground nutmeg, and ground ginger.
2. Blend the ingredients on high speed until smooth and creamy.
3. If the smoothie is too thick, you can add more almond milk, a little at a time, until you reach your desired consistency.
4. Add chia seeds to the blender and pulse a few times to mix them into the smoothie.
5. Taste the smoothie and add honey or maple syrup if you desire extra sweetness. Blend again to combine.

6. If you prefer a colder smoothie, add a handful of ice cubes and blend until they are fully incorporated.
7. Pour the Pumpkin Pie Protein Smoothie into glasses and garnish with a sprinkle of cinnamon or a dollop of Greek yogurt if desired.
8. Enjoy this delightful and protein-packed smoothie as a satisfying breakfast to kickstart your day.

Nutrition Information:
(Per serving)
- Calories: 220, Protein: 20g, Fat: 6g, Carbohydrates: 25g, Fiber: 7g, Sugar: 10g
Note: Nutrition Information may vary based on the specific brands and quantities of ingredients used. Adjustments can be made to suit individual dietary preferences and needs.

51. Breakfast Sandwich with Turkey Sausage

Start your day on a healthy and satisfying note with our delicious Breakfast Sandwich with Turkey Sausage. Packed with protein and flavor, this Weight Watchers-approved recipe will fuel your morning without compromising your wellness goals. The combination of lean turkey sausage, fluffy eggs, and whole-grain English muffins makes for a delightful breakfast that won't weigh you down.

Serving: Serves 2
Preparation Time: 15 minutes
Ready Time: 20 minutes

Ingredients:
- 4 turkey sausage patties (pre-cooked, preferably lean)
- 4 whole-grain English muffins, split and toasted
- 4 large eggs
- 2 slices reduced-fat cheddar cheese
- 1 tablespoon olive oil
- Salt and pepper to taste
- Optional toppings: sliced tomatoes, spinach, or avocado

Instructions:

1. Cook Turkey Sausage: In a skillet over medium heat, warm the pre-cooked turkey sausage patties for 2-3 minutes on each side until heated through.
2. Prepare Eggs: In the same skillet, add olive oil. Crack the eggs into the pan, season with salt and pepper, and cook to your desired doneness (consider making them over-easy or poached for a gooey yolk).
3. Assemble Sandwiches: Place a slice of reduced-fat cheddar cheese on the bottom half of each toasted English muffin. Top with a cooked turkey sausage patty and a cooked egg. Add optional toppings like sliced tomatoes, spinach, or avocado if desired. Finish with the top half of the English muffin.
4. Serve: Plate the breakfast sandwiches and serve immediately while the cheese is still melty and the eggs are warm.

Nutrition Information:
Per Serving (1 sandwich):
- Calories: 350, Total Fat: 16g, Saturated Fat: 4g, Trans Fat: 0g, Cholesterol: 210mg, Sodium: 650mg, Total Carbohydrates: 30g, Dietary Fiber: 5g, Sugars: 2g, Protein: 22g
Note: Nutrition Information is approximate and may vary based on specific brands and quantities of ingredients used.

52. Breakfast Chia Pudding with Berries

Start your day on a delicious and nutritious note with this Breakfast Chia Pudding with Berries—a perfect addition to your repertoire of Popular Weight Watchers Breakfast Recipes. Packed with the goodness of chia seeds and the vibrant flavors of fresh berries, this wholesome dish not only satisfies your taste buds but also supports your health and wellness goals. Easy to prepare and Weight Watchers-friendly, it's a delightful way to kickstart your morning.

Serving: 4 servings
Preparation Time: 10 minutes
Ready Time: 4 hours (overnight soaking required)

Ingredients:
- 1/2 cup chia seeds

- 2 cups unsweetened almond milk (or any milk of your choice)
- 1 teaspoon vanilla extract
- 1 tablespoon maple syrup or honey (optional, adjust to taste)
- 1 cup mixed berries (strawberries, blueberries, raspberries)
- 1 tablespoon sliced almonds (optional, for garnish)

Instructions:
1. In a mixing bowl, combine the chia seeds, almond milk, vanilla extract, and maple syrup or honey. Whisk the ingredients together until well combined.
2. Allow the mixture to rest for a few minutes, and then whisk again to prevent clumping.
3. Cover the bowl and refrigerate the chia seed mixture for at least 4 hours or preferably overnight. This allows the chia seeds to absorb the liquid and create a pudding-like consistency.
4. Before serving, give the pudding a good stir to ensure an even texture.
5. Wash and prepare the mixed berries. If using strawberries, slice them for easy mixing.
6. In serving glasses or bowls, layer the chia pudding with the mixed berries.
7. Optionally, garnish with sliced almonds for added crunch and texture.
8. Serve chilled and enjoy a flavorful and satisfying Breakfast Chia Pudding with Berries!

Nutrition Information:
(Per serving)
- Calories: 180, Total Fat: 8g, Saturated Fat: 1g, Trans Fat: 0g, Cholesterol: 0mg, Sodium: 80mg, Total Carbohydrates: 22g, Dietary Fiber: 10g, Sugars: 7g, Protein: 5g
Note: Nutrition Information may vary based on specific ingredients used.

53. Whole Wheat Waffles with Fresh Berries

Start your day on a wholesome note with these delightful Whole Wheat Waffles topped with a burst of fresh berries. This breakfast recipe is not only a treat for your taste buds but also a smart choice for those following the Weight Watchers program. Packed with fiber and antioxidants, these waffles offer a guilt-free indulgence that's both satisfying and nutritious.

Serving: Makes 4 servings
Preparation Time: 15 minutes
Ready Time: 25 minutes

Ingredients:
- 1 cup whole wheat flour
- 1 tablespoon sugar
- 1 teaspoon baking powder
- 1/2 teaspoon baking soda
- 1/4 teaspoon salt
- 1 cup low-fat buttermilk
- 1 large egg
- 2 tablespoons unsalted butter, melted
- 1 teaspoon vanilla extract
- Cooking spray
- 1 cup fresh mixed berries (strawberries, blueberries, raspberries)

Instructions:
1. Preheat Waffle Iron:
Preheat your waffle iron according to the manufacturer's instructions.
2. Prepare Dry **Ingredients:**
In a large bowl, whisk together the whole wheat flour, sugar, baking powder, baking soda, and salt.
3. Combine Wet **Ingredients:**
In another bowl, whisk together the buttermilk, egg, melted butter, and vanilla extract.
4. Mix Batter:
Pour the wet ingredients into the dry ingredients and stir until just combined. Be careful not to overmix; a few lumps are okay.
5. Cook Waffles:
Lightly coat the waffle iron with cooking spray. Pour the batter onto the preheated waffle iron, spreading it evenly. Close the lid and cook according to the manufacturer's instructions until the waffles are golden brown and crisp.
6. Serve:

Remove the waffles from the iron and place them on serving plates. Top each waffle with a generous handful of fresh mixed berries.
7. Optional:
Drizzle with a touch of maple syrup or a dollop of Greek yogurt for added flavor.

Nutrition Information:
Per Serving (1 waffle with berries):
- Calories: 230, Total Fat: 8g, Saturated Fat: 4g, Cholesterol: 55mg, Sodium: 400mg, Total Carbohydrates: 33g, Dietary Fiber: 5g, Sugars: 7g, Protein: 8g

These Whole Wheat Waffles with Fresh Berries are not only a delicious way to start your day but also a healthy choice for those mindful of their wellness journey with Weight Watchers. Enjoy a satisfying breakfast that keeps you energized throughout the morning!

54. Oatmeal with Sliced Peaches

Start your day on a deliciously healthy note with this satisfying and nutritious Weight Watchers breakfast – Oatmeal with Sliced Peaches. Packed with the wholesome goodness of oats and the natural sweetness of fresh peaches, this recipe is a delightful way to kickstart your morning while keeping you on track with your wellness goals.

Serving: 2 servings
Preparation Time: 5 minutes
Ready Time: 10 minutes

Ingredients:
- 1 cup old-fashioned rolled oats
- 2 cups water
- 1/4 teaspoon salt
- 1 cup fresh peaches, sliced
- 1 tablespoon honey (optional, for added sweetness)
- 1/2 teaspoon vanilla extract
- 1/2 teaspoon ground cinnamon
- 1/4 cup skim milk or a non-dairy alternative

Instructions:
1. In a medium saucepan, bring 2 cups of water to a boil.
2. Stir in the rolled oats and salt, then reduce the heat to medium-low. Cook the oats, stirring occasionally, for about 5 minutes or until they reach your desired consistency.
3. While the oats are cooking, slice the fresh peaches.
4. Once the oats are cooked, remove the saucepan from the heat and stir in the vanilla extract, ground cinnamon, and honey (if using).
5. Divide the cooked oatmeal between two bowls.
6. Top each bowl with sliced peaches and a drizzle of skim milk or your preferred non-dairy alternative.
7. Garnish with additional peach slices or a sprinkle of cinnamon if desired.
8. Serve warm and enjoy this wholesome and Weight Watchers-friendly breakfast.

Nutrition Information
(per serving):
- Calories: 250, Protein: 7g, Carbohydrates: 51g, Dietary Fiber: 7g, Sugars: 15g, Fat: 3g, Saturated Fat: 0.5g, Cholesterol: 0mg, Sodium: 300mg

Note: Nutrition Information is approximate and may vary based on specific ingredients used. Adjust honey and milk quantities based on personal preference and dietary needs.

55. Veggie and Egg Breakfast Tostadas

Start your day on a delicious and healthy note with these Veggie and Egg Breakfast Tostadas. Packed with fresh vegetables, protein-rich eggs, and vibrant flavors, these tostadas make for a satisfying and weight-conscious breakfast. The combination of nutrient-dense ingredients will keep you energized throughout the morning while helping you stay on track with your Weight Watchers goals. Get ready to savor a tasty and guilt-free start to your day!

Serving: Makes 4 tostadas
Preparation Time: 15 minutes
Ready Time: 20 minutes

Ingredients:
- 4 whole grain tostada shells
- 4 large eggs
- 1 cup cherry tomatoes, halved
- 1/2 cup bell peppers, diced (assorted colors)
- 1/2 cup red onion, finely chopped
- 1/2 cup black beans, drained and rinsed
- 1/4 cup fresh cilantro, chopped
- 1 avocado, sliced
- 1 tablespoon olive oil
- Salt and pepper to taste
- Optional toppings: salsa, Greek yogurt, hot sauce

Instructions:
1. In a skillet over medium heat, add olive oil. Sauté the diced bell peppers and red onion until softened, about 3-4 minutes.
2. Add the cherry tomatoes and black beans to the skillet. Cook for an additional 2-3 minutes, allowing the tomatoes to soften slightly.
3. Push the vegetables to the side of the skillet, creating space for the eggs. Crack each egg into the skillet, keeping them separate. Cook the eggs to your preferred doneness, either scrambled or sunny-side-up.
4. While the eggs are cooking, warm the tostada shells in a toaster or oven according to package instructions.
5. Assemble the tostadas: Place a tostada shell on a plate and layer with the sautéed vegetables and beans. Top with a cooked egg.
6. Garnish each tostada with sliced avocado, fresh cilantro, and season with salt and pepper to taste.
7. Optional: Add a dollop of Greek yogurt, salsa, or hot sauce for an extra burst of flavor.

Nutrition Information:
(Per Serving)
- Calories: 280, Protein: 14g, Fat: 16g, Carbohydrates: 22g, Fiber: 7g, Sugar: 3g, Sodium: 250mg

Note: Nutrition Information is approximate and may vary based on specific ingredients and portion sizes. Adjust quantities to meet your dietary preferences and needs.

56. Blueberry Almond Protein Pancakes

Start your day on a healthy and delicious note with these Blueberry Almond Protein Pancakes! Packed with wholesome ingredients and a generous dose of protein, these pancakes are perfect for those following the Weight Watchers program. The delightful combination of blueberries and almonds not only adds a burst of flavor but also provides essential nutrients to kick-start your morning. Enjoy a guilt-free breakfast that satisfies your taste buds and supports your wellness goals.

Serving: Makes 4 servings (2 pancakes per serving)
Preparation Time: 15 minutes
Ready Time: 25 minutes

Ingredients:
- 1 cup whole wheat flour
- 1/2 cup almond flour
- 1/4 cup vanilla protein powder
- 1 tablespoon baking powder
- 1/2 teaspoon salt
- 1 cup unsweetened almond milk
- 2 large eggs
- 2 tablespoons maple syrup
- 1 teaspoon vanilla extract
- 1/2 cup fresh blueberries
- 1/4 cup sliced almonds, toasted (for garnish)
- Cooking spray

Instructions:
1. In a large mixing bowl, whisk together the whole wheat flour, almond flour, protein powder, baking powder, and salt.
2. In a separate bowl, beat the eggs and then add the almond milk, maple syrup, and vanilla extract. Mix well.
3. Pour the wet ingredients into the dry ingredients and stir until just combined. Be careful not to overmix; a few lumps are okay.
4. Gently fold in the fresh blueberries.
5. Preheat a griddle or non-stick skillet over medium heat. Lightly coat with cooking spray.

6. Pour 1/4 cup of batter onto the griddle for each pancake. Cook until bubbles form on the surface, then flip and cook the other side until golden brown.
7. Repeat until all the batter is used.
8. Serve the pancakes warm, topped with a sprinkle of toasted sliced almonds and an extra drizzle of maple syrup if desired.

Nutrition Information
(per serving):
- Calories: 280, Protein: 12g, Carbohydrates: 36g, Dietary Fiber: 6g, Sugars: 8g, Fat: 11g, Saturated Fat: 1g, Cholesterol: 95mg, Sodium: 560mg
Note: Nutrition Information is approximate and may vary based on specific ingredients used. Adjustments can be made to suit individual dietary needs.

57. Breakfast Baked Potato

Start your day on a delicious and nutritious note with our Breakfast Baked Potato—a wholesome twist to the classic baked potato that's perfect for those following the Weight Watchers program. Packed with flavor and low in SmartPoints, this breakfast option is a delightful way to kickstart your morning. The combination of a perfectly baked potato, protein-rich eggs, and vibrant veggies makes it a satisfying and healthy choice for a hearty breakfast.

Serving: Serves 2
Preparation Time: 15 minutes
Ready Time: 40 minutes

Ingredients:
- 2 large baking potatoes
- 4 large eggs
- 1 cup cherry tomatoes, halved
- 1/2 cup red bell pepper, diced
- 1/4 cup green onions, thinly sliced
- 1/4 cup reduced-fat cheddar cheese, shredded
- 1 tablespoon olive oil

- Salt and pepper to taste
- Fresh parsley, chopped (for garnish)

Instructions:
1. Preheat the Oven:
Preheat your oven to 400°F (200°C).
2. Prepare the Potatoes:
Scrub the baking potatoes thoroughly and pierce them with a fork. Rub the potatoes with olive oil, sprinkle with salt, and place them on a baking sheet.
3. Bake the Potatoes:
Bake the potatoes in the preheated oven for about 40 minutes or until they are tender when pierced with a fork.
4. Prepare the Filling:
While the potatoes are baking, heat a non-stick skillet over medium heat. Add the cherry tomatoes, red bell pepper, and green onions. Sauté for 3-5 minutes until the vegetables are slightly softened.
5. Cook the Eggs:
In the same skillet, create wells in the vegetable mixture and crack the eggs into the wells. Season with salt and pepper. Cook the eggs to your desired level of doneness.
6. Assemble the Breakfast Baked Potatoes:
Once the potatoes are baked, slice them open and fluff the insides with a fork. Divide the sautéed vegetables and eggs equally between the two potatoes. Top with shredded cheddar cheese.
7. Garnish and Serve:
Garnish with fresh parsley and serve hot. The creamy potatoes, runny eggs, and colorful veggies create a delicious and satisfying breakfast.

Nutrition Information
(per serving):
- Calories: 320, Protein: 15g, Carbohydrates: 40g, Fiber: 5g, Sugars: 4g, Fat: 12g, Saturated Fat: 3.5g, Cholesterol: 370mg, Sodium: 320mg

Enjoy this Breakfast Baked Potato as a delightful and guilt-free way to start your day!

58. Greek Yogurt and Mango Parfait

Indulge in a delightful and nutritious morning treat with our Greek Yogurt and Mango Parfait—a perfect addition to your weight watchers' breakfast repertoire. This vibrant parfait combines the creamy goodness of Greek yogurt with the tropical sweetness of fresh mango, creating a satisfying and wholesome start to your day. Packed with protein and vitamins, this parfait not only satisfies your taste buds but also supports your wellness journey.

Serving: Serves 2
Preparation Time: 15 minutes
Ready Time: 15 minutes

Ingredients:
- 1 cup non-fat Greek yogurt
- 1 ripe mango, peeled and diced
- 2 tablespoons honey
- 1/2 cup granola (choose a low-sugar or sugar-free option for a lighter version)
- 1/4 cup sliced almonds
- 1 teaspoon chia seeds
- Fresh mint leaves for garnish (optional)

Instructions:
1. In a bowl, mix the non-fat Greek yogurt with honey until well combined. This will be the creamy base of your parfait.
2. In serving glasses or bowls, layer the Greek yogurt mixture with diced mango, alternating until the glass is filled.
3. Sprinkle a layer of granola over the yogurt and mango mixture. The granola adds a delightful crunch and additional fiber.
4. Repeat the layers until you reach the top of the glass, finishing with a layer of diced mango on top.
5. Garnish with sliced almonds and a sprinkle of chia seeds for added texture and nutritional benefits.
6. Optionally, top with fresh mint leaves for a burst of freshness and visual appeal.
7. Serve immediately and enjoy this satisfying and flavorful Greek Yogurt and Mango Parfait!

Nutrition Information:
Per Serving (1 parfait):

- Calories: 250, Total Fat: 7g, Saturated Fat: 1g, Trans Fat: 0g, Cholesterol: 5mg, Sodium: 50mg, Total Carbohydrates: 38g, Dietary Fiber: 5g, Sugars: 25g, Protein: 13g

Note: Nutrition Information is approximate and may vary based on specific ingredients used. Adjust quantities based on your dietary needs and preferences.

59. Spinach and Feta Breakfast Strata

Start your day on a delicious and nutritious note with our Spinach and Feta Breakfast Strata. This flavorful and satisfying dish is not only a crowd-pleaser but also a perfect addition to your Weight Watchers breakfast routine. Packed with the goodness of spinach, feta, and other wholesome ingredients, this strata is a delightful way to fuel your morning while keeping track of your points.

Serving: Serves 8
Preparation Time: 15 minutes
Ready Time: 1 hour 15 minutes

Ingredients:
- 8 slices whole wheat bread, cubed
- 1 cup fresh spinach, chopped
- 1 cup cherry tomatoes, halved
- 1 cup feta cheese, crumbled
- 1/2 cup red onion, finely chopped
- 1/4 cup fresh basil, chopped
- 6 large eggs
- 2 cups skim milk
- 1 teaspoon Dijon mustard
- 1/2 teaspoon garlic powder
- Salt and pepper to taste
- Cooking spray

Instructions:
1. Preheat the oven to 350°F (175°C). Lightly coat a 9x13-inch baking dish with cooking spray.

2. In a large bowl, combine the cubed bread, chopped spinach, cherry tomatoes, feta cheese, red onion, and fresh basil. Toss the ingredients together until evenly distributed in the bowl.
3. In a separate bowl, whisk together the eggs, skim milk, Dijon mustard, garlic powder, salt, and pepper until well combined.
4. Pour the egg mixture over the bread and vegetable mixture. Gently toss everything together, ensuring that the bread absorbs the liquid.
5. Transfer the mixture to the prepared baking dish, spreading it evenly. Let it sit for about 10 minutes to allow the bread to absorb the liquid.
6. Bake in the preheated oven for 50-60 minutes or until the strata is set in the middle and golden brown on top.
7. Allow the strata to cool for a few minutes before slicing and serving.

Nutrition Information:
Note: Nutrition Information may vary based on specific ingredients and brands used.
- Serving Size: 1 slice
- Calories: 220, Total Fat: 8g, Saturated Fat: 4g, Cholesterol: 140mg, Sodium: 450mg, Total Carbohydrates: 25g, Dietary Fiber: 4g, Sugars: 5g, Protein: 12g

Enjoy a tasty and guilt-free breakfast with our Spinach and Feta Breakfast Strata, perfect for anyone on a Weight Watchers journey or anyone looking for a wholesome start to their day.

60. Cinnamon Apple Oatmeal

Start your day on a delicious and nutritious note with our Cinnamon Apple Oatmeal, a perfect addition to your Popular Weight Watchers Breakfast Recipes collection. This wholesome dish combines the heartiness of oats, the sweetness of apples, and the warmth of cinnamon for a comforting breakfast that won't derail your wellness journey.

Serving: 4 servings
Preparation Time: 10 minutes
Ready Time: 20 minutes

Ingredients:
- 1 cup old-fashioned rolled oats

- 2 cups water
- 1 cup skim milk (or any milk of your choice)
- 2 medium apples, peeled, cored, and diced
- 2 tablespoons brown sugar (adjust to taste)
- 1 teaspoon ground cinnamon
- 1/4 teaspoon salt
- 1 teaspoon vanilla extract
- Optional toppings: sliced almonds, raisins, or a dollop of non-fat Greek yogurt

Instructions:
1. In a medium saucepan, combine the rolled oats, water, and milk. Bring to a gentle boil over medium heat, stirring occasionally to prevent sticking.
2. Once the mixture starts boiling, reduce the heat to low and add the diced apples, brown sugar, cinnamon, and salt. Stir well to combine.
3. Simmer the oatmeal for about 10-15 minutes or until the oats are tender and the apples are soft. Stir in the vanilla extract during the last few minutes of cooking.
4. Remove the saucepan from the heat and let the oatmeal sit for a couple of minutes to thicken.
5. Serve the Cinnamon Apple Oatmeal warm, dividing it into four bowls. Top each bowl with your choice of optional toppings, such as sliced almonds, raisins, or a dollop of non-fat Greek yogurt.

Nutrition Information
(per serving):
- Calories: 220, Total Fat: 2g, Saturated Fat: 0.5g, Trans Fat: 0g, Cholesterol: 0mg, Sodium: 160mg, Total Carbohydrates: 47g, Dietary Fiber: 6g, Sugars: 20g, Protein: 6g

Enjoy a guilt-free breakfast that's not only satisfying but also contributes to your overall well-being on your Weight Watchers journey.

61. Breakfast Quesadilla with Turkey Bacon

Start your day on a delicious and healthy note with our Breakfast Quesadilla with Turkey Bacon! This flavorful recipe is a perfect addition to your Weight Watchers breakfast routine, combining the satisfying taste of turkey bacon with the goodness of veggies and eggs, all wrapped in a warm tortilla. With a balanced mix of protein and veggies, this breakfast quesadilla is a tasty way to kickstart your morning while staying on track with your weight loss goals.

Serving: 2 Quesadillas
Preparation Time: 15 minutes
Ready Time: 20 minutes

Ingredients:
- 4 whole wheat or low-carb tortillas
- 4 large eggs, beaten
- 8 slices turkey bacon, cooked and crumbled
- 1 cup cherry tomatoes, diced
- 1/2 cup red bell pepper, diced
- 1/4 cup green onions, thinly sliced
- 1 cup reduced-fat shredded cheddar cheese
- Salt and pepper to taste
- Cooking spray

Instructions:
1. In a non-stick skillet, spray with cooking spray and scramble the eggs over medium heat until cooked through. Season with salt and pepper to taste.
2. On a separate skillet, cook the turkey bacon until crispy. Once cooked, crumble into bite-sized pieces.
3. Lay out the tortillas on a clean surface. Evenly distribute the scrambled eggs, crumbled turkey bacon, diced cherry tomatoes, red bell pepper, green onions, and shredded cheddar cheese among the tortillas.
4. Fold the tortillas in half, pressing gently to secure the filling.
5. In the same skillet used for eggs and bacon, place the filled tortillas and cook on both sides until the cheese is melted, and the tortillas are golden brown.
6. Remove from the skillet and let them cool slightly before slicing each quesadilla in half.
7. Serve warm and enjoy your delightful and satisfying Breakfast Quesadilla with Turkey Bacon!

Nutrition Information:

Note: Nutritional values may vary depending on specific brands and quantities used.
- Calories: Approximately 320 per serving, Protein: 20g, Carbohydrates: 25g, Fat: 15g, Fiber: 4g

Start your day the Weight Watchers way with this tasty and nutritious breakfast option that's sure to keep you energized and on track with your wellness goals!

62. Strawberry Banana Protein Smoothie

Start your day on a deliciously healthy note with our Strawberry Banana Protein Smoothie! Packed with the goodness of fresh fruits and a protein punch, this smoothie is not only a delightful treat for your taste buds but also a smart choice for those following the Weight Watchers program. Enjoy the sweet and tangy flavors while giving your body the fuel it needs to tackle the day ahead.

Serving: Makes 2 servings
Preparation Time: 10 minutes
Ready Time: 10 minutes

Ingredients:
- 1 cup fresh strawberries, hulled
- 1 ripe banana
- 1/2 cup plain Greek yogurt
- 1 scoop vanilla protein powder (check for Weight Watchers-friendly options)
- 1 cup unsweetened almond milk
- 1 tablespoon chia seeds
- Ice cubes (optional)

Instructions:
1. Prepare the
Ingredients:
Wash the strawberries, hull them, and peel the ripe banana.
2. Blend the Fruits:
In a blender, combine the fresh strawberries, banana, plain Greek yogurt, and vanilla protein powder.

3. Add Almond Milk:
Pour in the unsweetened almond milk to the blender. This not only adds a creamy texture but also keeps the smoothie light and refreshing.
4. Incorporate Chia Seeds:
Add chia seeds to the mix for an extra boost of fiber and omega-3 fatty acids.
5. Blend Until Smooth:
Blend all the ingredients until you achieve a smooth and creamy consistency. If you prefer a colder smoothie, you can also add a handful of ice cubes before blending.
6. Serve and Enjoy:
Pour the smoothie into glasses and savor the delicious blend of strawberries and bananas. It's a delightful and nutritious way to kickstart your day.

Nutrition Information
(per serving):
- Calories: XXX, Protein: XXX grams, Carbohydrates: XXX grams, Fiber: XXX grams, Sugar: XXX grams, Fat: XXX grams, Saturated Fat: XXX grams, Cholesterol: XXX milligrams, Sodium: XXX milligrams
Note: Nutrition Information may vary based on specific brands of ingredients and protein powder used. Adjustments may be needed based on individual dietary preferences.

63. Peanut Butter and Chocolate Overnight Oats

Kickstart your day with a delicious and satisfying breakfast that won't derail your weight watchers journey. Our Peanut Butter and Chocolate Overnight Oats combine the rich flavors of peanut butter and chocolate with the convenience of overnight preparation. Packed with wholesome ingredients, this recipe is a delightful and nutritious way to fuel your morning while staying on track with your weight watchers goals.
Serving: 1
Preparation Time: 10 minutes
Ready Time: Overnight (at least 6 hours)

Ingredients:
- 1/2 cup old-fashioned oats

- 1/2 cup unsweetened almond milk (or any milk of your choice)
- 1 tablespoon chia seeds
- 1 tablespoon powdered peanut butter
- 1 tablespoon cocoa powder
- 1 tablespoon sugar-free maple syrup
- 1/2 teaspoon vanilla extract
- A pinch of salt
- 1 tablespoon dark chocolate chips (optional, for garnish)
- 1 tablespoon chopped peanuts (optional, for garnish)

Instructions:
1. In a mason jar or airtight container, combine the oats, almond milk, chia seeds, powdered peanut butter, cocoa powder, sugar-free maple syrup, vanilla extract, and a pinch of salt.
2. Stir the mixture until well combined, ensuring that the ingredients are evenly distributed.
3. Seal the jar or container and refrigerate overnight or for at least 6 hours. This allows the oats to absorb the liquid and soften.
4. The next morning, give the oats a good stir. If the mixture is too thick, you can add a splash of almond milk until you reach your desired consistency.
5. Top the oats with dark chocolate chips and chopped peanuts for an extra layer of flavor and texture.
6. Enjoy your Peanut Butter and Chocolate Overnight Oats straight from the jar or transfer them to a bowl. These oats can be enjoyed cold or warmed up in the microwave for a cozy breakfast.

Nutrition Information:
Note: Nutrition values are approximate and may vary based on specific ingredients used.
- Calories: 350, Protein: 12g, Carbohydrates: 45g, Dietary Fiber: 10g, Sugars: 5g, Fat: 15g, Saturated Fat: 3g, Cholesterol: 0mg, Sodium: 150mg

64. Breakfast Stuffed Bell Peppers

Start your day with a burst of flavor and a healthy dose of satisfaction with these Breakfast Stuffed Bell Peppers. Packed with wholesome ingredients and perfectly balanced for those following the Weight

Watchers program, this recipe is a delightful way to kickstart your morning. The vibrant bell peppers serve as the edible bowl for a delicious mixture of eggs, lean protein, and veggies, making it a filling and nutritious breakfast option.

Serving: 4 servings
Preparation Time: 15 minutes
Ready Time: 35 minutes

Ingredients:
- 4 large bell peppers, halved and seeds removed
- 1 teaspoon olive oil
- 1 onion, finely chopped
- 2 cloves garlic, minced
- 1 cup lean turkey sausage, cooked and crumbled
- 1 cup cherry tomatoes, halved
- 1 cup spinach, chopped
- 6 large eggs
- Salt and pepper to taste
- 1/2 cup reduced-fat cheddar cheese, shredded
- Fresh parsley, chopped (for garnish)

Instructions:
1. Preheat the oven to 375°F (190°C).
2. Place the halved bell peppers on a baking sheet, cut side up.
3. In a skillet over medium heat, add olive oil. Sauté the chopped onion until translucent, then add minced garlic and cook for an additional 1-2 minutes.
4. Add the cooked turkey sausage, cherry tomatoes, and chopped spinach to the skillet. Stir and cook for 2-3 minutes until the spinach wilts.
5. In a separate bowl, beat the eggs and season with salt and pepper.
6. Pour the beaten eggs into the skillet with the sausage and vegetable mixture. Cook, stirring gently, until the eggs are just set.
7. Spoon the egg mixture evenly into the halved bell peppers.
8. Sprinkle shredded cheddar cheese over the top of each stuffed pepper.
9. Bake in the preheated oven for 20-25 minutes or until the peppers are tender and the cheese is melted and bubbly.
10. Remove from the oven, garnish with fresh parsley, and serve hot.

Nutrition Information

(per serving):
- Calories: 230, Protein: 18g, Fat: 13g, Carbohydrates: 12g, Fiber: 3g, Sugar: 6g, Sodium: 480mg
Note: Nutrition Information may vary based on specific ingredients used and portion sizes.

65. Veggie and Egg Breakfast Muffins

Start your day right with these delicious Veggie and Egg Breakfast Muffins, a perfect addition to your Popular Weight Watchers Breakfast Recipes. Packed with wholesome ingredients and bursting with flavor, these muffins are not only satisfying but also a healthy way to kickstart your morning. Plus, they're easy to make and great for meal prep!

Serving: Makes 12 muffins
Preparation Time: 15 minutes
Ready Time: 30 minutes

Ingredients:
- 6 large eggs
- 1 cup egg whites
- 1 cup cherry tomatoes, diced
- 1 cup spinach, chopped
- 1/2 cup bell peppers, finely diced (mix of colors)
- 1/2 cup red onion, finely chopped
- 1/2 cup reduced-fat feta cheese, crumbled
- 1 teaspoon olive oil
- 1 teaspoon dried oregano
- 1/2 teaspoon garlic powder
- Salt and pepper to taste
- Cooking spray

Instructions:
1. Preheat the oven to 350°F (175°C). Grease a muffin tin with cooking spray.
2. In a medium-sized skillet, heat the olive oil over medium heat. Add the red onion and sauté until softened, about 3-4 minutes.

3. Add the cherry tomatoes, bell peppers, and spinach to the skillet. Cook until the vegetables are tender and the spinach is wilted, about 2-3 minutes.
4. In a large mixing bowl, whisk together the eggs and egg whites. Add the sautéed vegetables, feta cheese, dried oregano, garlic powder, salt, and pepper. Mix until well combined.
5. Pour the egg mixture evenly into the muffin tin, filling each cup about two-thirds full.
6. Bake in the preheated oven for 15-20 minutes or until the muffins are set and slightly golden on top.
7. Allow the muffins to cool in the tin for a few minutes before transferring them to a wire rack to cool completely.

Nutrition Information:
Per serving (1 muffin):
- Calories: 80, Total Fat: 4g, Saturated Fat: 1.5g, Cholesterol: 125mg, Sodium: 150mg, Total Carbohydrates: 4g, Dietary Fiber: 1g, Sugars: 1g, Protein: 8g

These Veggie and Egg Breakfast Muffins are not only a delicious and satisfying way to start your day but also a smart choice for those following the Weight Watchers program. Enjoy a tasty and nutritious breakfast without compromising your health and wellness goals!

66. Whole Wheat Pancakes with Mixed Berries

Start your day on a delicious and nutritious note with these Whole Wheat Pancakes with Mixed Berries. Packed with the goodness of whole wheat flour and a burst of flavor from a medley of fresh berries, these pancakes are a perfect addition to your Weight Watchers breakfast routine. They're light, fluffy, and guilt-free, making them an ideal choice for those mindful of their points.

Serving: Makes approximately 8 pancakes
Preparation Time: 15 minutes
Ready Time: 25 minutes

Ingredients:
- 1 cup whole wheat flour

- 1 tablespoon baking powder
- 1/2 teaspoon salt
- 1 cup skim milk
- 1 large egg
- 2 tablespoons maple syrup (plus extra for serving)
- 1 teaspoon vanilla extract
- Cooking spray
- 1 cup mixed berries (strawberries, blueberries, raspberries)

Instructions:

1. In a large mixing bowl, whisk together the whole wheat flour, baking powder, and salt.
2. In a separate bowl, beat the egg and then add the milk, maple syrup, and vanilla extract. Mix well.
3. Pour the wet ingredients into the dry ingredients and stir until just combined. Do not overmix; a few lumps are okay.
4. Heat a non-stick griddle or skillet over medium heat and lightly coat with cooking spray.
5. For each pancake, ladle about 1/4 cup of batter onto the griddle. Cook until bubbles form on the surface, then flip and cook the other side until golden brown.
6. Remove the pancakes from the griddle and keep warm. Repeat until all the batter is used.
7. In the same skillet, briefly cook the mixed berries until they are warmed through, about 2-3 minutes.
8. Serve the pancakes topped with the mixed berries and an extra drizzle of maple syrup if desired.

Nutrition Information:

Per Serving (2 pancakes with berries):
- Calories: 220, Total Fat: 2g, Saturated Fat: 0.5g, Cholesterol: 35mg, Sodium: 400mg, Total Carbohydrates: 45g, Dietary Fiber: 5g, Sugars: 12g, Protein: 7g

Enjoy these Whole Wheat Pancakes with Mixed Berries as a delightful and satisfying breakfast that won't derail your Weight Watchers journey.

67. Breakfast Tacos with Avocado

Start your day with a burst of flavor and nutrition with these Breakfast Tacos with Avocado. Packed with protein, healthy fats, and fresh ingredients, these tacos are a delicious way to kick-start your morning while staying on track with your weight loss goals.

Serving: Makes 4 servings (2 tacos per serving)
Preparation Time: 15 minutes
Ready Time: 20 minutes

Ingredients:
- 8 small corn tortillas
- 4 large eggs
- 1 ripe avocado, sliced
- 1 cup black beans, drained and rinsed
- 1 cup cherry tomatoes, halved
- 1/2 cup diced red onion
- 1/4 cup chopped cilantro
- 1 lime, cut into wedges
- Salt and pepper to taste
- Optional: hot sauce or salsa for topping

Instructions:
1. Prepare the Ingredients: Warm the corn tortillas in a dry skillet over medium heat until soft and pliable. Keep them warm wrapped in a clean kitchen towel. Slice the avocado, halve the cherry tomatoes, dice the red onion, and chop the cilantro.
2. Cook the Eggs: In a non-stick skillet over medium heat, crack the eggs and cook to your desired doneness (scrambled, fried, or poached). Season with salt and pepper while cooking.
3. Assemble the Tacos: Lay out the warmed tortillas. Divide the cooked eggs among them, followed by the avocado slices, black beans, cherry tomatoes, red onion, and cilantro. Squeeze a lime wedge over each taco for a zesty kick.
4. Add Optional Toppings: If desired, drizzle with hot sauce or spoon over some salsa for extra flavor.
5. Serve: Arrange the assembled tacos on a serving platter and serve immediately while warm.

Nutrition Information
(per serving - 2 tacos):

- Calories: 320, Total Fat: 12g, Saturated Fat: 2g, Cholesterol: 190mg, Sodium: 230mg
- Total Carbohydrate: 42g, Dietary Fiber: 10g, Sugars: 3g, Protein: 14g

Note: Nutrition Information is approximate and may vary based on specific ingredients used and portion sizes.

Enjoy these Breakfast Tacos with Avocado as a flavorful and satisfying way to start your day, all while keeping your weight loss goals in check!

68. Caramelized Banana Protein Pancakes

Start your day off right with these delectable caramelized banana protein pancakes! Packed with protein and bursting with the natural sweetness of bananas, these pancakes are not only a treat for your taste buds but also a perfect choice for a healthy breakfast. Whether you're on a weight management journey or simply looking for a delicious morning meal, these pancakes will satisfy your cravings without compromising on nutrition.

Serving: 2 servings
Preparation time: 10 minutes
Ready time: 20 minutes

Ingredients:
- 2 ripe bananas, mashed
- 2 eggs
- 1/4 cup unsweetened almond milk (or any milk of choice)
- 1 scoop vanilla protein powder
- 1/2 cup oat flour
- 1 teaspoon baking powder
- 1/2 teaspoon cinnamon
- 1 tablespoon coconut oil (for cooking)
- Optional toppings: sliced bananas, a drizzle of sugar-free caramel sauce, a sprinkle of chopped nuts

Instructions:
1. In a mixing bowl, combine the mashed bananas, eggs, and almond milk. Whisk together until well blended.

2. Add the vanilla protein powder, oat flour, baking powder, and cinnamon to the wet ingredients. Stir until the batter is smooth and evenly mixed.
3. Heat a non-stick skillet or griddle over medium heat and add half of the coconut oil.
4. Pour about 1/4 cup of batter onto the skillet for each pancake. Cook until bubbles form on the surface, then flip and cook the other side until golden brown.
5. Repeat with the remaining batter, adding more coconut oil to the skillet as needed.
6. Once all the pancakes are cooked, serve them hot, topped with sliced bananas, a drizzle of sugar-free caramel sauce, and a sprinkle of chopped nuts if desired.

Nutrition Information
(per serving):
- Calories: 320, Protein: 18g, Fat: 11g, Carbohydrates: 40g, Fiber: 6g, Sugar: 14g
- WW SmartPoints (blue/purple/green): 8/8/9

69. Breakfast Salad with Poached Egg

Start your day on a healthy note with this vibrant Breakfast Salad with Poached Egg. Packed with nutritious ingredients and a perfectly poached egg on top, this dish is not only delicious but also a great choice for those following the Weight Watchers program. With fresh veggies, protein-rich eggs, and a zesty dressing, this salad will energize you for the day ahead while keeping you on track with your wellness goals.
Serving: 1 serving
Preparation time: 10 minutes
Ready time: 15 minutes

Ingredients:
For the Salad:
- 2 cups mixed greens (spinach, arugula, or your choice)
- 1/2 cup cherry tomatoes, halved
- 1/4 cup cucumber, sliced
- 1/4 cup bell pepper, diced

- 1/4 avocado, sliced
- 1 tablespoon red onion, thinly sliced

For the Poached Egg:
- 1 large egg
- Water (for poaching)

For the Dressing:
- 1 tablespoon extra-virgin olive oil
- 1 tablespoon fresh lemon juice
- 1/2 teaspoon Dijon mustard
- Salt and pepper to taste

Instructions:
1. Prepare the mixed greens by washing and drying them thoroughly. Place them in a large salad bowl.
2. Add the cherry tomatoes, cucumber slices, diced bell pepper, sliced avocado, and thinly sliced red onion on top of the greens.
3. In a small bowl, whisk together the extra-virgin olive oil, fresh lemon juice, Dijon mustard, salt, and pepper to create the dressing.
4. Drizzle the dressing over the salad ingredients and toss gently to coat everything evenly.
5. For the poached egg, fill a small saucepan with water and bring it to a gentle simmer over medium heat.
6. Crack the egg into a small bowl or ramekin. Using a spoon, create a gentle whirlpool in the simmering water and carefully slide the egg into the center of the whirlpool. Poach for about 3-4 minutes for a slightly runny yolk or longer for a firmer yolk.
7. Remove the poached egg with a slotted spoon and place it on top of the prepared salad.
8. Serve the Breakfast Salad with Poached Egg immediately and enjoy the burst of flavors and textures!

Nutrition Information:
- Calories: 250, Total Fat: 18g, Saturated Fat: 3g, Cholesterol: 186mg, Sodium: 170mg, Total Carbohydrates: 15g, Dietary Fiber: 7g, Sugars: 4g, Protein: 10g

Note: Nutrition Information is approximate and may vary based on specific ingredients used. Adjustments can be made based on individual dietary needs.

70. Greek Yogurt and Berry Parfait

Start your day on a delicious and healthy note with this delightful Greek Yogurt and Berry Parfait. Packed with the goodness of protein-rich Greek yogurt and the natural sweetness of fresh berries, this parfait is not only a treat for your taste buds but also a smart choice for those following a Weight Watchers plan. The combination of creamy yogurt, vibrant berries, and a touch of sweetness creates a breakfast that's both satisfying and figure-friendly.

Serving: Serves 2
Preparation Time: 15 minutes
Ready Time: 15 minutes

Ingredients:
- 1 cup non-fat Greek yogurt
- 1 tablespoon honey or maple syrup (optional)
- 1 teaspoon vanilla extract
- 1 cup mixed berries (strawberries, blueberries, raspberries)
- 1/4 cup granola (choose a low-sugar or sugar-free option for a Weight Watchers-friendly version)
- Fresh mint leaves for garnish (optional)

Instructions:
1. In a bowl, mix the Greek yogurt with honey (or maple syrup) and vanilla extract. Adjust sweetness to taste.
2. Wash and prepare the berries, slicing strawberries if desired.
3. In serving glasses or bowls, begin layering the parfait. Start with a spoonful of the sweetened Greek yogurt at the bottom.
4. Add a layer of mixed berries on top of the yogurt.
5. Sprinkle a layer of granola over the berries.
6. Repeat the layers until the glass is filled, finishing with a dollop of yogurt on the top.
7. Garnish with fresh mint leaves if desired.
8. Serve immediately and enjoy this delightful and Weight Watchers-friendly breakfast treat!

Nutrition Information:
Per serving (serves 2):

- Calories: 220, Protein: 15g, Fat: 2g, Carbohydrates: 40g, Fiber: 5g, Sugar: 20g, Sodium: 80mg

Note: Nutrition Information may vary based on specific brands and quantities used. Adjustments can be made to suit individual dietary preferences and requirements.

71. Spinach and Tomato Breakfast Pizza

Start your day on a delicious and healthy note with this Spinach and Tomato Breakfast Pizza! Packed with vibrant flavors and nutritious ingredients, this recipe is a perfect addition to your Popular Weight Watchers Breakfast Recipes. The combination of fresh spinach, juicy tomatoes, and savory cheese on a light and fluffy crust will satisfy your morning cravings while keeping you on track with your wellness goals.

Serving: Makes 4 servings
Preparation Time: 15 minutes
Ready Time: 25 minutes

Ingredients:
- 1 pre-made whole wheat pizza crust (about 12 inches in diameter)
- 1 cup fresh spinach, chopped
- 1 cup cherry tomatoes, sliced
- 1/2 cup reduced-fat shredded mozzarella cheese
- 4 large eggs
- 1/4 cup skim milk
- 1/4 teaspoon salt
- 1/4 teaspoon black pepper
- 1/4 teaspoon garlic powder
- Cooking spray

Instructions:
1. Preheat the oven to 425°F (220°C).
2. Place the pizza crust on a baking sheet lined with parchment paper. Lightly spray the crust with cooking spray to help it crisp up in the oven.
3. In a bowl, whisk together the eggs, skim milk, salt, black pepper, and garlic powder until well combined.

4. Spread the chopped spinach evenly over the pizza crust, followed by the sliced cherry tomatoes.
5. Sprinkle the shredded mozzarella cheese over the vegetables.
6. Pour the egg mixture evenly over the top of the pizza.
7. Carefully transfer the baking sheet to the preheated oven and bake for 18-20 minutes or until the crust is golden brown and the eggs are set.
8. Remove from the oven and let it cool for a few minutes before slicing.
9. Serve slices of the Spinach and Tomato Breakfast Pizza warm, and enjoy a nutritious and satisfying breakfast!

Nutrition Information:
(Per serving)
- Calories: 280, Total Fat: 9g, Saturated Fat: 3g, Cholesterol: 190mg, Sodium: 560mg, Total Carbohydrates: 34g, Dietary Fiber: 4g, Sugars: 2g, Protein: 17g
Note: Nutrition Information is approximate and may vary based on specific ingredients used. Adjustments can be made based on individual dietary preferences and needs.

72. Blueberry Protein Waffles

Start your day on a delicious and nutritious note with our Blueberry Protein Waffles! Packed with protein and bursting with the sweet flavor of blueberries, these waffles are a perfect addition to your Weight Watchers breakfast routine. Indulge in a guilt-free breakfast that will keep you satisfied and energized throughout the morning.

Serving: Makes 4 servings
Preparation Time: 15 minutes
Ready Time: 25 minutes

Ingredients:
- 1 cup whole wheat flour
- 1 scoop vanilla protein powder
- 1 tablespoon baking powder
- 1/2 teaspoon cinnamon
- 1/4 teaspoon salt
- 1 cup unsweetened almond milk

- 1 large egg
- 2 tablespoons maple syrup
- 1 teaspoon vanilla extract
- 1 cup fresh blueberries

Instructions:
1. Preheat your waffle iron according to the manufacturer's instructions.
2. In a large mixing bowl, whisk together the whole wheat flour, protein powder, baking powder, cinnamon, and salt.
3. In a separate bowl, whisk together the almond milk, egg, maple syrup, and vanilla extract until well combined.
4. Pour the wet ingredients into the dry ingredients and stir until just combined. Be careful not to overmix; a few lumps are okay.
5. Gently fold in the fresh blueberries into the batter.
6. Lightly grease the waffle iron with non-stick cooking spray.
7. Pour enough batter onto the preheated waffle iron to cover the waffle grid. Close the lid and cook until the waffle is golden brown and crisp.
8. Repeat with the remaining batter.
9. Serve the Blueberry Protein Waffles warm, topped with additional fresh blueberries or a drizzle of maple syrup if desired.

Nutrition Information
(per serving):
- Calories: 250, Protein: 12g, Carbohydrates: 40g, Dietary Fiber: 6g, Sugars: 10g, Fat: 5g, Saturated Fat: 1g, Cholesterol: 45mg, Sodium: 480mg

These Blueberry Protein Waffles are not only delicious but also a fantastic way to start your day on a healthy and satisfying note. Enjoy a breakfast that supports your wellness journey without compromising on flavor!

73. Breakfast Burrito with Turkey Sausage

Start your day with a burst of flavor and a healthy dose of protein with this delicious Breakfast Burrito featuring lean turkey sausage. Packed with vibrant vegetables, savory spices, and wrapped in a warm tortilla, this Weight Watchers-friendly recipe will satisfy your morning cravings without compromising your wellness goals. Enjoy a hearty, satisfying breakfast that's both wholesome and delicious.

Serving: Makes 4 servings
Preparation Time: 15 minutes
Ready Time: 25 minutes

Ingredients:
- 1 pound lean turkey sausage, crumbled
- 1 tablespoon olive oil
- 1 onion, finely diced
- 1 bell pepper, diced (any color of your choice)
- 1 cup cherry tomatoes, halved
- 1 cup spinach, chopped
- 8 large eggs, beaten
- 1/4 cup skim milk
- Salt and pepper to taste
- 4 whole wheat or low-carb tortillas
- 1/2 cup reduced-fat shredded cheddar cheese
- Salsa and Greek yogurt (optional, for serving)

Instructions:
1. In a large skillet, heat olive oil over medium heat. Add the crumbled turkey sausage and cook until browned, breaking it apart with a spoon as it cooks.
2. Add diced onion and bell pepper to the skillet. Sauté until the vegetables are tender.
3. Stir in cherry tomatoes and chopped spinach. Cook for an additional 2-3 minutes until the tomatoes are slightly softened and the spinach wilts.
4. In a bowl, whisk together the eggs and skim milk. Season with salt and pepper to taste. Pour the egg mixture into the skillet with the sausage and vegetables.
5. Gently scramble the eggs until they are fully cooked and mixed with the sausage and vegetables.
6. Warm the tortillas according to package instructions.
7. Assemble the burritos by spooning the egg and sausage mixture onto each tortilla. Sprinkle with shredded cheddar cheese.
8. Fold in the sides of the tortilla and roll it up tightly to form a burrito.
9. Serve the breakfast burritos with salsa and Greek yogurt if desired.

Nutrition Information:
(Per serving)
- Calories: 350, Total Fat: 18g, Saturated Fat: 5g, Cholesterol: 290mg, Sodium: 600mg, Total Carbohydrates: 20g, Dietary Fiber: 4g, Sugars: 3g, Protein: 26g

Indulge in this hearty Breakfast Burrito with Turkey Sausage guilt-free, knowing you've started your day on a nutritious and delicious note.

74. Breakfast Stuffed Mushrooms

Start your day with a burst of flavor and a boost of nutrition with these Breakfast Stuffed Mushrooms. Packed with wholesome ingredients and designed with Weight Watchers in mind, this recipe combines the earthy richness of mushrooms with a delightful blend of breakfast favorites. Whether you're watching your weight or simply looking for a delicious morning meal, these stuffed mushrooms are a perfect choice to kickstart your day on a healthy note.

Serving: Makes 4 servings
Preparation Time: 15 minutes
Ready Time: 30 minutes

Ingredients:
- 8 large mushrooms, cleaned and stems removed
- 1 teaspoon olive oil
- 1/4 cup onion, finely chopped
- 1/4 cup red bell pepper, finely chopped
- 2 cloves garlic, minced
- 4 turkey sausage links, casings removed
- 1 cup spinach, chopped
- 4 large eggs
- Salt and pepper to taste
- 1/4 cup reduced-fat feta cheese, crumbled
- Fresh parsley for garnish (optional)

Instructions:
1. Preheat the oven to 375°F (190°C).

2. Place the cleaned mushrooms on a baking sheet, cap side down, and bake for 10 minutes to help remove excess moisture. Remove from the oven and set aside.
3. In a large skillet, heat olive oil over medium heat. Add chopped onion, red bell pepper, and minced garlic. Sauté until the vegetables are softened, about 3-4 minutes.
4. Add the turkey sausage to the skillet, breaking it up with a spatula as it cooks. Cook until browned and cooked through.
5. Stir in the chopped spinach and cook until wilted. Season with salt and pepper to taste.
6. Carefully spoon the sausage and vegetable mixture into each mushroom cap, creating a well in the center.
7. Crack an egg into each mushroom cap, placing it in the well created by the sausage and vegetables.
8. Sprinkle crumbled feta cheese over the top of each stuffed mushroom.
9. Bake in the preheated oven for 15-20 minutes or until the egg whites are set but the yolks are still runny.
10. Garnish with fresh parsley if desired and serve hot.

Nutrition Information
(per serving):
- Calories: 180, Protein: 16g, Carbohydrates: 6g, Dietary Fiber: 2g, Sugars: 2g, Total Fat: 10g, Saturated Fat: 3g, Cholesterol: 205mg, Sodium: 360mg

75. Peanut Butter and Jelly Protein Pancakes

Start your day on a delicious and nutritious note with these Peanut Butter and Jelly Protein Pancakes. Packed with the goodness of protein and the classic flavors of peanut butter and jelly, these pancakes are a perfect addition to your weight watchers breakfast repertoire. They not only satisfy your cravings but also keep you energized throughout the morning.

Serving: Makes approximately 4 servings
Preparation Time: 15 minutes
Ready Time: 25 minutes

Ingredients:
- 1 cup whole wheat flour
- 1 scoop vanilla protein powder
- 1 tablespoon baking powder
- 1/2 teaspoon salt
- 1 cup skim milk
- 1/4 cup creamy peanut butter
- 2 tablespoons honey
- 2 large eggs
- 1 teaspoon vanilla extract
- Cooking spray
- 1/2 cup sugar-free strawberry or grape jelly (for topping)

Instructions:
1. In a large mixing bowl, whisk together the whole wheat flour, protein powder, baking powder, and salt.
2. In a separate microwave-safe bowl, warm the peanut butter and honey together until they become smooth and easy to mix. Stir well.
3. Add the peanut butter mixture, milk, eggs, and vanilla extract to the dry ingredients. Mix until just combined. Be careful not to overmix; it's okay if there are a few lumps.
4. Preheat a griddle or non-stick skillet over medium heat. Lightly coat with cooking spray.
5. Pour 1/4 cup of batter onto the griddle for each pancake. Cook until bubbles form on the surface, then flip and cook the other side until golden brown.
6. Repeat until all the batter is used, keeping pancakes warm in a low oven if necessary.
7. Serve the pancakes topped with a dollop of sugar-free strawberry or grape jelly for that classic peanut butter and jelly flavor.

Nutrition Information
(per serving):
- Calories: 280, Protein: 16g, Carbohydrates: 32g, Dietary Fiber: 4g, Sugars: 11g, Fat: 10g, Saturated Fat: 2g, Cholesterol: 90mg, Sodium: 530mg

Note: Nutrition Information is approximate and may vary based on specific ingredients and serving sizes. Adjust quantities according to your dietary needs.

76. Oatmeal with Sliced Strawberries

Start your day on a deliciously healthy note with our "Oatmeal with Sliced Strawberries" – a perfect addition to your Popular Weight Watchers Breakfast Recipes. Packed with wholesome ingredients and bursting with flavor, this breakfast bowl is a delightful blend of fiber and fresh fruit to kickstart your day. Plus, it's Weight Watchers friendly, making it a smart choice for those looking to enjoy a satisfying breakfast while keeping an eye on their points.

Serving: This recipe serves 2.
Preparation Time: 10 minutes
Ready Time: 15 minutes

Ingredients:
- 1 cup old-fashioned rolled oats
- 2 cups water
- 1/4 teaspoon salt
- 1 cup sliced strawberries
- 2 tablespoons honey or maple syrup (optional)
- 1/4 cup chopped nuts (almonds, walnuts, or pecans)
- 1 teaspoon chia seeds (optional)
- 1/2 teaspoon vanilla extract
- 1 cup unsweetened almond milk or skim milk

Instructions:
1. In a medium saucepan, bring 2 cups of water to a boil.
2. Add the rolled oats and salt to the boiling water, stirring occasionally.
3. Reduce heat to medium-low and let the oats simmer for about 5-7 minutes or until they reach your desired consistency, stirring occasionally.
4. While the oats are cooking, wash and slice the strawberries.
5. Once the oats are cooked, remove the saucepan from heat and stir in the vanilla extract.
6. Divide the cooked oats into two bowls.
7. Top each bowl of oatmeal with sliced strawberries, chopped nuts, and chia seeds if using.
8. Drizzle with honey or maple syrup if desired.

9. Pour 1/2 cup of unsweetened almond milk or skim milk over each bowl.
10. Give it a gentle stir, and your delicious Oatmeal with Sliced Strawberries is ready to be enjoyed!

Nutrition Information:
(Per Serving)
- Calories: 300, Total Fat: 8g, Saturated Fat: 1g, Cholesterol: 0mg, Sodium: 150mg, Total Carbohydrates: 50g, Dietary Fiber: 8g, Sugars: 12g, Protein: 9g

Note: Nutrition Information may vary based on specific ingredients and brands used. Adjust quantities accordingly based on your dietary needs and preferences.

77. Veggie and Egg Breakfast Bowl

Start your day on a healthy and satisfying note with our Veggie and Egg Breakfast Bowl—a perfect addition to your weight watchers journey. Packed with nutritious vegetables and protein-rich eggs, this breakfast bowl not only satisfies your taste buds but also keeps you full and energized throughout the morning. The combination of fresh veggies and eggs creates a delicious and wholesome meal that is low in SmartPoints, making it an ideal choice for those following the Weight Watchers program.

Serving: 2 servings
Preparation Time: 15 minutes
Ready Time: 20 minutes

Ingredients:
- 4 large eggs
- 1 cup cherry tomatoes, halved
- 1 cup spinach, chopped
- 1/2 bell pepper, diced (any color)
- 1/2 onion, finely chopped
- 1 clove garlic, minced
- 1 tablespoon olive oil
- Salt and pepper to taste

- 1/2 teaspoon dried oregano
- 1/4 cup feta cheese, crumbled (optional)
- Fresh parsley for garnish (optional)

Instructions:
1. Heat olive oil in a non-stick skillet over medium heat.
2. Add chopped onions and garlic to the skillet, sautéing until they become translucent.
3. Add diced bell peppers and cherry tomatoes to the skillet, cooking for an additional 3-4 minutes until the vegetables are slightly softened.
4. Stir in chopped spinach and cook until wilted.
5. Create wells in the vegetable mixture and crack one egg into each well. Season the eggs with salt, pepper, and dried oregano.
6. Cover the skillet with a lid and let the eggs cook to your desired doneness. For a runny yolk, cook for about 3 minutes; for a firmer yolk, cook for 5-6 minutes.
7. Sprinkle crumbled feta cheese over the eggs and vegetables, if desired.
8. Garnish with fresh parsley and serve the Veggie and Egg Breakfast Bowl hot.

Nutrition Information:
(Per Serving)
- Calories: 220, Total Fat: 15g, Saturated Fat: 4g, Cholesterol: 370mg, Sodium: 320mg, Total Carbohydrates: 10g, Dietary Fiber: 3g, Sugars: 4g, Protein: 14g

Enjoy this delicious and nutritious breakfast bowl guilt-free as you embark on your weight loss journey with Weight Watchers!

78. Breakfast Tostadas with Avocado

Start your day on a delicious and healthy note with these Breakfast Tostadas with Avocado. Packed with nutritious ingredients and vibrant flavors, this recipe is a perfect addition to your collection of Weight Watchers breakfast options. The combination of crunchy tostadas, creamy avocado, and flavorful toppings will leave you satisfied and ready to take on the day.

Serving: Serves 4

Preparation Time: 15 minutes
Ready Time: 20 minutes

Ingredients:
- 4 corn tostadas
- 2 ripe avocados, peeled, pitted, and sliced
- 4 large eggs
- 1 cup cherry tomatoes, halved
- 1/4 cup red onion, finely chopped
- 1/4 cup fresh cilantro, chopped
- 1 lime, cut into wedges
- Salt and pepper to taste
- Cooking spray

Instructions:
1. Preheat the Oven: Preheat your oven to 375°F (190°C).
2. Prepare the Tostadas: Place the corn tostadas on a baking sheet and warm them in the preheated oven for about 5 minutes, or until they become crisp.
3. Cook the Eggs: While the tostadas are warming, heat a non-stick skillet over medium heat and lightly coat it with cooking spray. Crack the eggs into the skillet and cook to your preference (fried, scrambled, or poached).
4. Assemble the Tostadas: Place a warm tostada on each plate. Top with sliced avocado, cooked eggs, cherry tomatoes, red onion, and cilantro.
5. Season and Garnish: Season the tostadas with salt and pepper to taste. Garnish each tostada with a lime wedge for a burst of citrusy flavor.
6. Serve: These Breakfast Tostadas with Avocado are ready to be enjoyed. Serve them immediately while the tostadas are still crisp and the eggs are warm.

Nutrition Information
(per serving):
- Calories: 280, Protein: 10g, Carbohydrates: 20g, Dietary Fiber: 7g, Sugars: 2g, Fat: 18g, Saturated Fat: 3g, Cholesterol: 185mg, Sodium: 150mg

Note: Nutrition Information is approximate and may vary based on specific ingredients and portion sizes. Adjustments can be made to meet individual dietary preferences and needs.

79. Cinnamon Raisin Protein French Toast

Start your day on a delicious and nutritious note with our Cinnamon Raisin Protein French Toast. This Weight Watchers-friendly breakfast is a perfect blend of warm, comforting flavors and a protein boost to keep you satisfied throughout the morning. With the sweet aroma of cinnamon, the plump juiciness of raisins, and the added protein kick, this recipe is a delightful twist on a classic breakfast favorite.

Serving: Serves 4
Preparation Time: 15 minutes
Ready Time: 20 minutes

Ingredients:
- 8 slices of whole wheat bread (preferably low-point bread for Weight Watchers)
- 4 large eggs
- 1 cup unsweetened almond milk (or any milk of your choice)
- 1 scoop vanilla protein powder
- 1 teaspoon ground cinnamon
- 1/2 teaspoon vanilla extract
- 1/4 cup raisins
- Cooking spray or a pat of butter for the pan

Instructions:
1. In a mixing bowl, whisk together the eggs, almond milk, vanilla protein powder, ground cinnamon, and vanilla extract until well combined.
2. Stir in the raisins, ensuring they are evenly distributed throughout the mixture.
3. Preheat a non-stick skillet or griddle over medium heat and lightly coat it with cooking spray or butter.
4. Dip each slice of bread into the egg mixture, ensuring both sides are well-coated. Allow any excess to drip off.
5. Place the coated bread slices on the preheated skillet and cook for 2-3 minutes per side or until golden brown and cooked through.
6. Repeat the process until all the bread slices are cooked, adding more cooking spray or butter as needed.

7. Serve the Cinnamon Raisin Protein French Toast warm, topped with fresh fruit, a drizzle of sugar-free syrup, or a dollop of Greek yogurt if desired.

Nutrition Information
(per serving):
- Calories: XXX, Total Fat: XXg, Saturated Fat: Xg, Cholesterol: XXXmg, Sodium: XXXmg, Total Carbohydrates: XXg, Dietary Fiber: Xg, Sugars: XXg, Protein: XXg
(Note: Nutrition Information may vary based on specific brands of ingredients used and portion sizes.)

80. Breakfast Quiche with Spinach and Turkey Sausage

Start your day on a delicious and nutritious note with this flavorful Breakfast Quiche featuring the wholesome goodness of spinach and lean turkey sausage. Packed with protein and low in SmartPoints, it's a perfect addition to your Weight Watchers breakfast repertoire. This quiche is not only satisfying but also a delightful way to kickstart your morning routine.

Serving: Serves 6
Preparation Time: 15 minutes
Ready Time: 45 minutes

Ingredients:
- 1 pre-made pie crust (store-bought or homemade)
- 1 cup fresh spinach, chopped
- 1/2 cup turkey sausage, cooked and crumbled
- 1/2 cup cherry tomatoes, halved
- 1/2 cup reduced-fat shredded cheddar cheese
- 4 large eggs
- 1 cup skim milk
- 1/2 teaspoon salt
- 1/4 teaspoon black pepper
- 1/4 teaspoon garlic powder
- Cooking spray

Instructions:
1. Preheat your oven to 375°F (190°C).
2. Roll out the pie crust and press it into a greased 9-inch pie dish. Trim any excess crust hanging over the edges.
3. In a skillet over medium heat, sauté the chopped spinach until wilted. Remove excess moisture by pressing it between paper towels.
4. In the same skillet, cook the turkey sausage until browned and crumbly. Drain any excess fat.
5. In a mixing bowl, whisk together the eggs, milk, salt, black pepper, and garlic powder.
6. Spread the cooked spinach, turkey sausage, cherry tomatoes, and shredded cheddar cheese evenly over the pie crust.
7. Pour the egg mixture over the ingredients in the pie crust.
8. Bake in the preheated oven for 30-35 minutes or until the center is set and the top is golden brown.
9. Allow the quiche to cool for 10 minutes before slicing.

Nutrition Information:
Per Serving
- Calories: 250, Total Fat: 15g, Saturated Fat: 6g, Trans Fat: 0g, Cholesterol: 175mg, Sodium: 480mg, Total Carbohydrates: 17g, Dietary Fiber: 1g, Sugars: 2g, Protein: 13g
Note: Nutrition Information may vary based on specific brands and quantities of ingredients used. Adjustments may be necessary depending on your dietary needs.

81. Raspberry Chia Pudding

Indulge in a guilt-free and nutritious start to your day with our delectable Raspberry Chia Pudding, specially crafted for those following the Weight Watchers program. This vibrant and satisfying breakfast is not only a treat for your taste buds but also a wholesome choice to keep you energized throughout the morning. Packed with the goodness of chia seeds and the delightful sweetness of raspberries, this recipe is a perfect blend of flavor and wellness.

Serving: Makes 4 servings

Preparation Time: 15 minutes
Ready Time: 4 hours (including chilling time)

Ingredients:
- 1 cup fresh raspberries
- 1/4 cup maple syrup (adjust to taste)
- 1 teaspoon vanilla extract
- 1/2 cup chia seeds
- 2 cups unsweetened almond milk (or any milk of your choice)
- Optional toppings: additional raspberries, sliced almonds, mint leaves

Instructions:
1. Prepare the Raspberry Puree:
- In a blender, combine fresh raspberries, maple syrup, and vanilla extract. Blend until smooth.
- Strain the raspberry puree through a fine mesh sieve to remove seeds. Set aside.
2. Mix Chia Seeds and Almond Milk:
- In a medium-sized bowl, whisk together chia seeds and almond milk until well combined.
- Let the mixture sit for 5-10 minutes, stirring occasionally to prevent clumping.
3. Combine Raspberry Puree with Chia Mixture:
- Gently fold the raspberry puree into the chia seed mixture until evenly distributed.
- Taste and adjust sweetness by adding more maple syrup if desired.
4. Refrigerate to Set:
- Divide the mixture into four serving jars or bowls.
- Cover and refrigerate for at least 4 hours or overnight until the pudding has a thick, pudding-like consistency.
5. Serve and Enjoy:
- Before serving, garnish with additional raspberries, sliced almonds, or mint leaves for an extra burst of freshness.

Nutrition Information
(per serving):
- Calories: 180, Total Fat: 8g, Saturated Fat: 1g, Trans Fat: 0g, Cholesterol: 0mg, Sodium: 70mg, Total Carbohydrates: 25g, Dietary Fiber: 10g, Sugars: 10g, Protein: 5g

Note: Nutrition Information may vary based on specific ingredients and brands used.

82. Greek Yogurt and Honey Parfait

Start your day on a delicious and nutritious note with our Greek Yogurt and Honey Parfait—a delightful addition to your Popular Weight Watchers Breakfast Recipes. Packed with protein, probiotics, and the natural sweetness of honey, this parfait is a guilt-free treat that will satisfy your morning cravings while keeping you on track with your weight loss goals.

Serving: Serves 2
Preparation Time: 10 minutes
Ready Time: 10 minutes

Ingredients:
- 1 cup non-fat Greek yogurt
- 1 tablespoon honey (adjust to taste)
- 1/2 cup granola (choose a low-sugar option)
- 1 cup mixed berries (strawberries, blueberries, raspberries)

Instructions:
1. In a bowl, combine the non-fat Greek yogurt and honey. Mix well until the honey is evenly distributed throughout the yogurt.
2. In serving glasses or bowls, start layering the parfait. Begin with a spoonful of the honeyed Greek yogurt at the bottom.
3. Add a layer of granola on top of the yogurt. Ensure an even distribution for a perfect balance of textures.
4. Wash and prepare the mixed berries. Add a layer of berries on top of the granola, creating a vibrant and flavorful layer.
5. Repeat the layers until you reach the top of the serving glass or bowl. Finish with a dollop of Greek yogurt and a drizzle of honey for an extra touch of sweetness.
6. Garnish with a few fresh berries on top for an appealing presentation.
7. Serve immediately and enjoy the perfect blend of creamy yogurt, crunchy granola, and the burst of fruity goodness.

Nutrition Information:
- Calories: 250 per serving, Protein: 15g, Fat: 2g, Carbohydrates: 45g, Fiber: 6g, Sugar: 18g, Sodium: 80mg
Note: Nutrition Information is approximate and may vary based on specific ingredients used. Adjust honey and granola quantities based on personal preferences and Weight Watchers points.

83. Spinach and Feta Breakfast Quesadilla

Start your day on a nutritious and delicious note with our Spinach and Feta Breakfast Quesadilla. Packed with vibrant flavors, this Weight Watchers-friendly breakfast is the perfect way to kickstart your morning while keeping your wellness goals in check. The combination of wholesome spinach, creamy feta, and savory seasonings will make this quesadilla a breakfast favorite.

Serving: Makes 2 quesadillas
Preparation Time: 15 minutes
Ready Time: 20 minutes

Ingredients:
- 4 whole wheat tortillas (8-inch size)
- 2 cups fresh baby spinach, chopped
- 1 cup reduced-fat feta cheese, crumbled
- 1 medium tomato, diced
- 1/4 cup red onion, finely chopped
- 1 teaspoon olive oil
- 1/2 teaspoon garlic powder
- 1/2 teaspoon dried oregano
- Salt and pepper to taste
- Cooking spray

Instructions:
1. Prepare the Filling:
- In a skillet, heat olive oil over medium heat. Add chopped spinach and cook until wilted, about 2-3 minutes. Season with garlic powder, dried oregano, salt, and pepper.
- Remove the skillet from heat and set aside the spinach mixture.

2. Assemble the Quesadillas:
- Lay out the whole wheat tortillas on a clean surface.
- Divide the cooked spinach evenly among two tortillas, spreading it evenly over one half of each tortilla.
- Sprinkle crumbled feta cheese over the spinach on each tortilla.
- Add diced tomatoes and chopped red onions on top of the feta.
3. Fold and Cook:
- Fold the empty half of each tortilla over the filling, creating a half-moon shape.
- Heat a non-stick skillet over medium heat and coat with cooking spray.
- Place the quesadillas in the skillet and cook for 2-3 minutes per side, or until the tortillas are golden brown and the cheese is melted.
4. Serve:
- Remove from the skillet and let them cool for a minute before slicing each quesadilla into halves.

Nutrition Information:
Per Serving (1 quesadilla)
- Calories: 320, Protein: 15g, Carbohydrates: 40g, Dietary Fiber: 8g, Sugars: 4g, Total Fat: 12g, Saturated Fat: 5g, Cholesterol: 20mg, Sodium: 650mg

These Spinach and Feta Breakfast Quesadillas are not only a tasty and satisfying breakfast option but also a nutritious choice to keep you fueled throughout the day. Enjoy guilt-free indulgence while staying on track with your Weight Watchers journey.

84. Blueberry Almond Baked Oatmeal

Start your day on a delicious and healthy note with our Blueberry Almond Baked Oatmeal, a perfect addition to your Popular Weight Watchers Breakfast Recipes collection. Packed with wholesome ingredients and bursting with the natural sweetness of blueberries, this baked oatmeal is a delightful and satisfying way to fuel your morning.

Serving: Serves 6
Preparation Time: 15 minutes
Ready Time: 45 minutes

Ingredients:
- 2 cups old-fashioned oats
- 1/2 cup slivered almonds
- 1 teaspoon baking powder
- 1/2 teaspoon cinnamon
- 1/4 teaspoon salt
- 1 1/2 cups unsweetened almond milk (or your choice of milk)
- 1/4 cup pure maple syrup
- 2 tablespoons almond butter
- 1 large egg
- 1 teaspoon vanilla extract
- 1 1/2 cups fresh or frozen blueberries

Instructions:
1. Preheat your oven to 350°F (175°C). Grease a baking dish with non-stick cooking spray.
2. In a large bowl, combine the oats, slivered almonds, baking powder, cinnamon, and salt. Mix well.
3. In a separate bowl, whisk together the almond milk, maple syrup, almond butter, egg, and vanilla extract until smooth and well combined.
4. Pour the wet ingredients into the bowl with the dry ingredients and stir until everything is evenly coated.
5. Gently fold in the blueberries, ensuring they are evenly distributed throughout the mixture.
6. Transfer the oatmeal mixture to the prepared baking dish, spreading it out evenly.
7. Bake in the preheated oven for 30-35 minutes or until the edges are golden brown and a toothpick inserted into the center comes out clean.
8. Allow the baked oatmeal to cool for a few minutes before slicing it into squares.

Nutrition Information:
(Per Serving)
- Calories: 280, Total Fat: 12g, Saturated Fat: 1g, Trans Fat: 0g, Cholesterol: 31mg, Sodium: 147mg, Total Carbohydrates: 37g, Dietary Fiber: 6g, Sugars: 12g, Protein: 8g

This Blueberry Almond Baked Oatmeal is not only a flavorful way to start your day but also a smart choice for those keeping an eye on their Weight Watchers points. Enjoy the wholesome goodness and delicious taste without compromising your wellness goals.

85. Veggie and Egg Breakfast Burrito

Start your day on a healthy and delicious note with this Veggie and Egg Breakfast Burrito, a perfect addition to your weight-conscious breakfast routine. Packed with nutritious vegetables and protein-rich eggs, this burrito will keep you satisfied and energized throughout the morning. It's a flavorful and satisfying choice for anyone looking to enjoy a tasty breakfast while keeping an eye on their weight.

Serving: Serves 2
Preparation Time: 15 minutes
Ready Time: 20 minutes

Ingredients:
- 4 whole wheat or low-carb tortillas
- 4 large eggs
- 1 cup diced bell peppers (assorted colors)
- 1 cup diced tomatoes
- 1/2 cup diced red onion
- 1/2 cup chopped fresh spinach
- 1/2 cup shredded reduced-fat cheddar cheese
- 1 teaspoon olive oil
- 1/2 teaspoon garlic powder
- Salt and pepper to taste
- Salsa and Greek yogurt for serving (optional)

Instructions:
1. Prepare the Vegetables:
- In a skillet, heat olive oil over medium heat. Add diced red onion, bell peppers, and tomatoes. Sauté until the vegetables are tender, about 5 minutes.
2. Scramble the Eggs:
- Push the sautéed vegetables to one side of the skillet. Crack the eggs into the empty side and scramble them until just set. Mix the eggs with the sautéed vegetables.
3. Add Spinach and Cheese:

- Stir in the chopped spinach, garlic powder, salt, and pepper. Cook for an additional 1-2 minutes until the spinach wilts and the ingredients are well combined. Sprinkle shredded cheddar cheese over the mixture and let it melt.

4. Warm the Tortillas:
- In a separate skillet or directly on a gas flame, warm each tortilla for about 10 seconds on each side until pliable.

5. Assemble the Burritos:
- Divide the egg and vegetable mixture evenly among the tortillas. Fold in the sides and roll up each tortilla to create a burrito.

6. Serve:
- Optionally, serve with salsa and a dollop of Greek yogurt for added flavor.

Nutrition Information:
(Per Serving)
- Calories: 300, Protein: 18g, Carbohydrates: 26g, Dietary Fiber: 6g, Sugars: 4g, Total Fat: 14g, Saturated Fat: 5g, Cholesterol: 370mg, Sodium: 450mg
- Vitamin D: 15%
- Calcium: 20%
- Iron: 15%
- Potassium: 25%

Enjoy this Veggie and Egg Breakfast Burrito guilt-free, as it not only satisfies your taste buds but also supports your weight-conscious lifestyle.

86. Mixed Berry Smoothie Bowl

Start your day on a deliciously healthy note with our Mixed Berry Smoothie Bowl! Packed with vibrant flavors and nutritional goodness, this breakfast recipe is a perfect choice for those following the Weight Watchers program. Bursting with the natural sweetness of mixed berries, this smoothie bowl is not only satisfying but also a delightful way to kickstart your morning routine. With a harmonious blend of ingredients, it's a guilt-free treat that will keep you energized and on track with your wellness goals.

Serving: This recipe serves 2.

Preparation Time: 10 minutes
Ready Time: 10 minutes

Ingredients:
- 1 cup frozen mixed berries (strawberries, blueberries, raspberries)
- 1 ripe banana
- 1/2 cup non-fat Greek yogurt
- 1/2 cup unsweetened almond milk
- 1 tablespoon chia seeds
- 1 tablespoon honey (optional, for added sweetness)
- 1/2 teaspoon vanilla extract
- Ice cubes (optional, for a thicker consistency)
- Fresh berries and granola for topping

Instructions:
1. In a blender, combine the frozen mixed berries, ripe banana, Greek yogurt, almond milk, chia seeds, honey (if using), and vanilla extract.
2. Blend the ingredients on high speed until smooth and creamy. If you prefer a thicker consistency, add ice cubes and blend again until well combined.
3. Pour the smoothie mixture into bowls.
4. Top the smoothie bowls with fresh berries and granola for added texture and flavor.
5. Serve immediately and enjoy your nutritious Mixed Berry Smoothie Bowl!

Nutrition Information:
Per Serving (without honey):
- Calories: 180, Protein: 8g, Carbohydrates: 38g, Dietary Fiber: 7g, Sugars: 19g, Fat: 2g, Saturated Fat: 0g, Cholesterol: 0mg, Sodium: 80mg
Note: Nutrition Information may vary based on specific brands and quantities of ingredients used.

87. Cottage Cheese and Fruit Bowl

Start your day on a delicious and nutritious note with this Cottage Cheese and Fruit Bowl—a perfect addition to your Popular Weight Watchers Breakfast Recipes. Packed with protein, vitamins, and a burst of natural sweetness, this breakfast bowl not only satisfies your taste buds but also supports your wellness goals. It's a delightful combination of creamy cottage cheese and vibrant fresh fruits that will leave you feeling energized and ready to tackle the day.

Serving: Serves 2
Preparation Time: 15 minutes
Ready Time: 15 minutes

Ingredients:
- 1 cup low-fat cottage cheese
- 1 cup strawberries, hulled and sliced
- 1 cup blueberries
- 1 medium banana, sliced
- 1 tablespoon honey (optional)
- 2 tablespoons chopped nuts (almonds, walnuts, or your choice)
- Fresh mint leaves for garnish

Instructions:
1. In a mixing bowl, spoon out the low-fat cottage cheese, ensuring a creamy base for your fruit bowl.
2. Add the sliced strawberries, blueberries, and banana to the cottage cheese. These colorful fruits not only add sweetness but also contribute essential vitamins and antioxidants.
3. Gently toss the fruits and cottage cheese together, ensuring an even distribution.
4. If you have a sweet tooth, drizzle a tablespoon of honey over the fruit and cheese mixture. This step is optional and can be adjusted based on your taste preferences.
5. Sprinkle the chopped nuts over the top for a satisfying crunch and an extra dose of healthy fats.
6. Divide the mixture into two serving bowls.
7. Garnish each bowl with fresh mint leaves for a burst of flavor and a visually appealing touch.
8. Your Cottage Cheese and Fruit Bowl is now ready to be enjoyed!

Nutrition Information
(per serving):

- Calories: 250, Protein: 18g, Carbohydrates: 35g, Dietary Fiber: 6g, Sugars: 22g, Fat: 6g, Saturated Fat: 1.5g, Cholesterol: 10mg, Sodium: 300mg

Note: Nutrition Information may vary based on specific ingredients used and can be adjusted based on individual dietary needs.

88. Peanut Butter and Banana Toast

Start your day on a delicious and nutritious note with our Peanut Butter and Banana Toast—a delightful twist to your morning routine. This weight watchers-friendly breakfast is not only satisfying but also a perfect balance of flavors. The creamy peanut butter pairs harmoniously with the sweetness of ripe bananas, creating a wholesome treat that will keep you energized throughout the day.

Serving: 2 servings
Preparation Time: 5 minutes
Ready Time: 7 minutes

Ingredients:
- 4 slices whole-grain bread
- 4 tablespoons natural peanut butter (unsweetened)
- 2 ripe bananas, thinly sliced
- 1 tablespoon honey (optional)
- Pinch of cinnamon (optional)

Instructions:
1. Toast the Bread: Place the slices of whole-grain bread in a toaster or toaster oven until they reach your desired level of crispiness.
2. Spread Peanut Butter: While the bread is still warm, spread 1 tablespoon of natural peanut butter onto each slice, ensuring an even layer.
3. Add Banana Slices: Arrange the thinly sliced bananas on top of the peanut butter-covered toast. Ensure an even distribution for a balanced bite.
4. Optional Sweetness: Drizzle a touch of honey over the banana slices for added sweetness. If you like, sprinkle a pinch of cinnamon for a warm, aromatic flavor.

5. Serve and Enjoy: Your Peanut Butter and Banana Toast is now ready to be enjoyed! Pair it with a cup of your favorite morning beverage for a satisfying and wholesome breakfast.

Nutrition Information
(per serving):
- Calories: 280, Total Fat: 12g, Saturated Fat: 2g, Cholesterol: 0mg, Sodium: 220mg, Total Carbohydrates: 38g, Dietary Fiber: 6g, Sugars: 14g, Protein: 8g

Note: Nutrition Information is approximate and may vary based on specific ingredients used. Adjustments can be made to fit individual dietary needs.

89. Breakfast Stuffed Peppers

Start your day on a delicious and healthy note with these Breakfast Stuffed Peppers! Packed with vibrant flavors and nutritious ingredients, this recipe is a perfect addition to your weight watchers' breakfast repertoire. The combination of colorful bell peppers, savory turkey sausage, and eggs creates a satisfying and low-point meal that will keep you energized throughout the morning.

Serving: Serves: 4
Preparation Time: Prep Time: 15 minutes
Ready Time: Ready in: 35 minutes

Ingredients:
- 4 large bell peppers, halved and seeds removed
- 1 pound lean turkey sausage, crumbled
- 1 cup cherry tomatoes, diced
- 1/2 cup red onion, finely chopped
- 1 cup spinach, chopped
- 1 teaspoon olive oil
- 8 large eggs
- Salt and pepper to taste
- 1/2 cup reduced-fat shredded cheddar cheese
- Fresh parsley for garnish (optional)

Instructions:
1. Preheat your oven to 375°F (190°C).
2. In a large skillet, heat the olive oil over medium heat. Add the turkey sausage and cook until browned, breaking it apart with a spoon as it cooks.
3. Add the red onion to the skillet and sauté until softened, about 3 minutes.
4. Stir in the cherry tomatoes and spinach, cooking until the spinach wilts and the tomatoes release their juices.
5. Place the bell pepper halves in a baking dish, cut side up.
6. Spoon the sausage and vegetable mixture evenly into each pepper half.
7. Carefully crack an egg into each pepper half, ensuring not to break the yolk.
8. Season each pepper with salt and pepper to taste.
9. Sprinkle the shredded cheddar cheese over the eggs.
10. Bake in the preheated oven for 20-25 minutes or until the egg whites are set, and the yolks are still slightly runny.
11. Garnish with fresh parsley if desired.
12. Serve warm and enjoy your delicious and satisfying Breakfast Stuffed Peppers!

Nutrition Information:
Per serving:
- Calories: 320, Total Fat: 15g, Saturated Fat: 5g, Cholesterol: 380mg, Sodium: 650mg, Total Carbohydrates: 15g, Dietary Fiber: 4g, Sugars: 7g, Protein: 28g

Note: Nutrition Information is approximate and may vary based on specific ingredients used.

90. Spinach and Mushroom Breakfast Pizza

Start your day with a burst of flavor and nutrition with this delightful Spinach and Mushroom Breakfast Pizza. Packed with wholesome ingredients, this recipe is not only delicious but also fits seamlessly into your Weight Watchers plan. The combination of fresh spinach, savory mushrooms, and a perfectly cooked egg creates a breakfast experience that's both satisfying and guilt-free.

Serving: Makes 4 servings
Preparation Time: 15 minutes
Ready Time: 25 minutes

Ingredients:
- 1 pound whole wheat pizza dough
- 1 cup part-skim mozzarella cheese, shredded
- 1 cup fresh spinach, chopped
- 1 cup mushrooms, sliced
- 4 large eggs
- 1 teaspoon olive oil
- 1 teaspoon garlic powder
- Salt and pepper to taste
- Optional: red pepper flakes for a spicy kick

Instructions:
1. Preheat Oven: Preheat your oven to 425°F (220°C).
2. Prepare Dough: Roll out the whole wheat pizza dough on a lightly floured surface, creating a thin crust. Place the rolled-out dough on a pizza stone or a baking sheet lined with parchment paper.
3. Saute Spinach and Mushrooms: In a skillet over medium heat, add olive oil. Sauté the sliced mushrooms until they are tender, and then add the chopped spinach. Cook until the spinach wilts. Season with garlic powder, salt, and pepper. Set aside.
4. Assemble Pizza: Spread the sautéed spinach and mushrooms evenly over the pizza dough. Sprinkle shredded mozzarella on top.
5. Create Wells for Eggs: Using the back of a spoon, make four wells in the pizza toppings. Carefully crack an egg into each well.
6. Bake: Transfer the pizza to the preheated oven and bake for 15-20 minutes or until the egg whites are set, and the yolks are still slightly runny.
7. Optional Spicy Kick: If you enjoy a bit of heat, sprinkle red pepper flakes over the pizza before serving.
8. Serve: Once the eggs are cooked to your liking, remove the pizza from the oven. Allow it to cool for a few minutes before slicing.

Nutrition Information:
(Per Serving)
- Calories: 350, Protein: 18g, Carbohydrates: 40g, Fiber: 6g, Sugars: 3g, Fat: 14g, Saturated Fat: 5g, Cholesterol: 195mg, Sodium: 550mg

This Spinach and Mushroom Breakfast Pizza is not only a delightful way to start your day but also a tasty addition to your Weight Watchers journey. Enjoy a guilt-free and satisfying breakfast that won't compromise your wellness goals.

91. Oat Bran and Raspberry Muffins

Start your day on a healthy and delicious note with these Oat Bran and Raspberry Muffins. Packed with fiber-rich oat bran and the vibrant sweetness of raspberries, these muffins are a delightful treat that won't compromise your commitment to a balanced breakfast. Created with Weight Watchers principles in mind, these muffins are a smart choice for those looking to kickstart their day with a tasty and nutritious breakfast.

Serving: Makes 12 muffins
Preparation Time: 15 minutes
Ready Time: 30 minutes

Ingredients:
- 1 cup oat bran
- 1 cup whole wheat flour
- 1/2 cup brown sugar, packed
- 1 teaspoon baking powder
- 1/2 teaspoon baking soda
- 1/4 teaspoon salt
- 1 cup non-fat Greek yogurt
- 2 large eggs
- 1/4 cup unsweetened applesauce
- 1 teaspoon vanilla extract
- 1 cup fresh raspberries

Instructions:
1. Preheat your oven to 375°F (190°C) and line a muffin tin with paper liners.
2. In a large mixing bowl, combine the oat bran, whole wheat flour, brown sugar, baking powder, baking soda, and salt. Mix well to ensure even distribution of dry ingredients.

3. In a separate bowl, whisk together the Greek yogurt, eggs, applesauce, and vanilla extract until smooth.

4. Pour the wet ingredients into the dry ingredients and gently fold until just combined. Be careful not to overmix; a few lumps are okay.

5. Gently fold in the fresh raspberries, ensuring they are evenly distributed throughout the batter.

6. Spoon the batter into the prepared muffin tin, filling each cup about two-thirds full.

7. Bake in the preheated oven for 15-18 minutes or until a toothpick inserted into the center of a muffin comes out clean.

8. Allow the muffins to cool in the tin for 5 minutes before transferring them to a wire rack to cool completely.

Nutrition Information:
Per Serving (1 muffin):
- Calories: 120, Total Fat: 1g, Saturated Fat: 0g, Cholesterol: 25mg, Sodium: 120mg, Total Carbohydrates: 24g, Dietary Fiber: 4g, Sugars: 8g, Protein: 5g

These Oat Bran and Raspberry Muffins make for a satisfying and guilt-free breakfast option, perfect for those following the Weight Watchers program. Enjoy the combination of hearty oat bran and the burst of flavor from fresh raspberries in every bite!

92. Sweet Potato Hash with Turkey Sausage

Start your day on a delicious and nutritious note with our Sweet Potato Hash with Turkey Sausage—a satisfying breakfast option that won't derail your weight loss journey. Packed with wholesome ingredients and bursting with flavors, this hearty dish is a perfect addition to your collection of Popular Weight Watchers Breakfast Recipes. With a balance of lean turkey sausage, vibrant sweet potatoes, and a medley of aromatic spices, this hash is a tasty way to kickstart your morning while keeping you on track with your wellness goals.

Serving: Serves 4
Preparation Time: 15 minutes
Ready Time: 30 minutes

Ingredients:
- 2 medium sweet potatoes, peeled and diced into 1/2-inch cubes
- 1 pound lean turkey sausage, casings removed
- 1 onion, finely chopped
- 1 bell pepper, diced
- 2 cloves garlic, minced
- 1 teaspoon smoked paprika
- 1/2 teaspoon ground cumin
- Salt and pepper to taste
- 1 tablespoon olive oil
- Fresh parsley, chopped (for garnish)

Instructions:
1. In a large skillet, heat olive oil over medium heat. Add diced sweet potatoes and cook until they begin to soften, about 8-10 minutes, stirring occasionally.
2. Add the lean turkey sausage to the skillet, breaking it apart with a spatula. Cook until the sausage is browned and cooked through, about 5-7 minutes.
3. Stir in the chopped onion, bell pepper, and minced garlic. Sauté until the vegetables are tender, about 5 minutes.
4. Sprinkle smoked paprika, ground cumin, salt, and pepper over the mixture. Stir well to combine, allowing the flavors to meld for another 2-3 minutes.
5. Once the sweet potatoes are fully cooked and slightly crispy, and the sausage and vegetables are well incorporated, remove the skillet from heat.
6. Garnish with freshly chopped parsley for a burst of freshness and color.

Nutrition Information:
Per serving:
- Calories: 320, Protein: 20g, Carbohydrates: 25g, Dietary Fiber: 4g, Sugars: 6g, Fat: 16g, Saturated Fat: 4g, Cholesterol: 60mg, Sodium: 680mg

Start your day with this flavorful Sweet Potato Hash with Turkey Sausage and embrace a breakfast that not only tastes delightful but also aligns with your weight watchers goals.

93. Breakfast Egg and Veggie Muffins

Start your day on a healthy and delicious note with these Breakfast Egg and Veggie Muffins. Packed with protein and loaded with colorful vegetables, these muffins are not only a treat for your taste buds but also a smart choice for those following the Weight Watchers program. Easy to make and perfectly portioned, these muffins are a great addition to your collection of popular Weight Watchers breakfast recipes.

Serving: Makes 12 muffins
Preparation Time: 15 minutes
Ready Time: 35 minutes

Ingredients:
- 8 large eggs
- 1/4 cup skim milk
- 1/2 teaspoon salt
- 1/4 teaspoon black pepper
- 1 cup diced bell peppers (assorted colors)
- 1/2 cup diced red onion
- 1/2 cup diced tomatoes
- 1/2 cup chopped spinach
- 1/4 cup finely chopped fresh parsley
- 1/2 cup shredded reduced-fat cheddar cheese

Instructions:
1. Preheat your oven to 350°F (175°C). Grease a muffin tin or line it with paper liners.
2. In a large bowl, whisk together the eggs, skim milk, salt, and black pepper until well combined.
3. Add the diced bell peppers, red onion, tomatoes, spinach, and fresh parsley to the egg mixture. Stir in the shredded cheddar cheese and mix until all ingredients are evenly distributed.
4. Pour the egg and veggie mixture into the prepared muffin tin, dividing it evenly among the cups.
5. Bake in the preheated oven for 20-25 minutes or until the muffins are set and the tops are golden brown.
6. Allow the muffins to cool for a few minutes in the tin before transferring them to a wire rack to cool completely.

Nutrition Information:
(Per serving - 1 muffin)
- Calories: 90, Total Fat: 5g, Saturated Fat: 2g, Cholesterol: 140mg, Sodium: 180mg, Total Carbohydrates: 4g, Dietary Fiber: 1g, Sugars: 2g, Protein: 8g
Note: Nutrition Information may vary based on specific ingredients and brands used.

94. Apple Cider Protein Pancakes

Start your day on a delicious and nutritious note with these Apple Cider Protein Pancakes. Packed with the wholesome goodness of apples and a protein boost, these pancakes are a perfect choice for a satisfying breakfast. Not only are they a treat for your taste buds, but they also align with the principles of Weight Watchers, making them an excellent option for those on a weight-conscious journey.

Serving: Makes 4 servings (2 pancakes per serving)
Preparation Time: 15 minutes
Ready Time: 25 minutes

Ingredients:
- 1 cup whole wheat flour
- 1 scoop vanilla protein powder
- 1 teaspoon baking powder
- 1/2 teaspoon ground cinnamon
- 1/4 teaspoon salt
- 1 cup unsweetened apple cider
- 1/4 cup unsweetened applesauce
- 1 large egg
- 1 tablespoon maple syrup
- 1 teaspoon vanilla extract
- Cooking spray for the pan

Instructions:
1. In a large mixing bowl, whisk together the whole wheat flour, protein powder, baking powder, cinnamon, and salt.

2. In a separate bowl, combine the apple cider, applesauce, egg, maple syrup, and vanilla extract. Mix well.
3. Add the wet ingredients to the dry ingredients, stirring until just combined. Be careful not to overmix; a few lumps are okay.
4. Heat a non-stick skillet or griddle over medium heat and lightly coat with cooking spray.
5. Pour 1/4 cup of batter onto the skillet for each pancake. Cook until bubbles form on the surface, then flip and cook the other side until golden brown.
6. Repeat until all the batter is used.
7. Serve the pancakes warm, topped with fresh apple slices or a drizzle of additional maple syrup if desired.

Nutrition Information
(per serving):
- Calories: 220, Protein: 12g, Carbohydrates: 38g, Dietary Fiber: 5g, Sugars: 10g, Fat: 3g, Saturated Fat: 1g, Cholesterol: 45mg, Sodium: 310mg
- Vitamin D: 1mcg
- Calcium: 120mg
- Iron: 2mg
- Potassium: 250mg

These Apple Cider Protein Pancakes offer a delightful blend of flavors and textures while keeping your breakfast both wholesome and satisfying. Enjoy guilt-free mornings with a plateful of these delicious pancakes!

95. Quinoa and Black Bean Breakfast Bowl

Start your day with a delicious and nutritious Quinoa and Black Bean Breakfast Bowl, a perfect addition to your Popular Weight Watchers Breakfast Recipes. Packed with protein, fiber, and flavor, this hearty breakfast bowl will keep you satisfied and energized throughout the morning. It's a delightful combination of quinoa, black beans, and fresh vegetables that will make your breakfast both enjoyable and healthy.

Serving: Serves 2
Preparation Time: 15 minutes

Ready Time: 25 minutes

Ingredients:
- 1 cup quinoa, rinsed
- 2 cups water
- 1 can (15 oz) black beans, drained and rinsed
- 1 cup cherry tomatoes, halved
- 1/2 cucumber, diced
- 1/4 cup red onion, finely chopped
- 1/4 cup fresh cilantro, chopped
- 1 avocado, sliced
- 2 tablespoons olive oil
- 1 tablespoon lime juice
- 1 teaspoon ground cumin
- Salt and pepper to taste
- Optional toppings: poached eggs, hot sauce

Instructions:
1. In a medium saucepan, combine the quinoa and water. Bring to a boil, then reduce heat to low, cover, and simmer for 15 minutes or until the quinoa is cooked and water is absorbed.
2. While the quinoa is cooking, prepare the black beans by heating them in a small saucepan over medium heat. Add cumin, salt, and pepper to taste. Stir well and cook until heated through.
3. In a large mixing bowl, combine the cooked quinoa, black beans, cherry tomatoes, cucumber, red onion, and cilantro.
4. In a small bowl, whisk together the olive oil and lime juice. Pour the dressing over the quinoa mixture and toss until well combined.
5. Divide the mixture into two bowls. Top each bowl with sliced avocado and any optional toppings you prefer, such as poached eggs or hot sauce.
6. Serve immediately and enjoy your wholesome Quinoa and Black Bean Breakfast Bowl!

Nutrition Information:
(Per serving)
- Calories: 450, Protein: 15g, Fat: 20g, Carbohydrates: 55g, Fiber: 12g, Sugar: 4g, Sodium: 350mg

Note: Nutrition Information is approximate and may vary based on specific ingredients used. Adjust quantities to meet your dietary preferences and needs.

96. Greek Yogurt and Honey Waffles

Start your day on a delightful and healthy note with these Greek Yogurt and Honey Waffles. Packed with protein-rich Greek yogurt and the natural sweetness of honey, these waffles are not only a delicious treat but also a perfect addition to your weight watchers' breakfast repertoire. Indulge guilt-free in the crispy exterior and fluffy interior of these waffles that will leave you satisfied and energized for the day ahead.

Serving: Makes 4 servings (2 waffles per serving)
Preparation Time: 15 minutes
Ready Time: 25 minutes

Ingredients:
- 1 cup whole wheat flour
- 1/2 cup rolled oats
- 1 tablespoon baking powder
- 1/2 teaspoon salt
- 1 cup non-fat Greek yogurt
- 1/2 cup skim milk
- 2 large eggs
- 2 tablespoons honey
- 1 teaspoon vanilla extract
- Cooking spray (for waffle iron)

Instructions:
1. Preheat your waffle iron according to the manufacturer's instructions.
2. In a large mixing bowl, combine the whole wheat flour, rolled oats, baking powder, and salt.
3. In a separate bowl, whisk together the Greek yogurt, skim milk, eggs, honey, and vanilla extract until well combined.
4. Pour the wet ingredients into the dry ingredients and stir until just combined. Be careful not to overmix; a few lumps are okay.
5. Lightly coat the waffle iron with cooking spray.
6. Spoon the batter onto the preheated waffle iron, spreading it evenly to cover the surface. Close the lid and cook until the waffles are golden brown and crisp.

7. Carefully remove the waffles and repeat the process until all the batter is used.
8. Serve the waffles warm, drizzled with an extra touch of honey if desired.

Nutrition Information
(per serving):
- Calories: 280, Protein: 17g, Carbohydrates: 45g, Fiber: 6g, Sugars: 10g, Fat: 4g, Saturated Fat: 1g, Cholesterol: 95mg, Sodium: 550mg
Note: Nutrition Information is approximate and may vary based on specific ingredients used.

97. Green Breakfast Smoothie

Start your day on a healthy note with this refreshing Green Breakfast Smoothie, a perfect addition to our collection of Popular Weight Watchers Breakfast Recipes. Packed with nutritious ingredients, this smoothie not only satisfies your taste buds but also supports your wellness journey. It's a delicious and low-point option that will keep you energized throughout the morning.

Serving: 2 servings
Preparation Time: 10 minutes
Ready Time: 10 minutes

Ingredients:
- 1 cup fresh spinach leaves, washed
- 1/2 cucumber, peeled and sliced
- 1/2 green apple, cored and chopped
- 1/2 ripe banana
- 1/2 cup non-fat Greek yogurt
- 1 tablespoon chia seeds
- 1 tablespoon honey (optional, for added sweetness)
- 1 cup unsweetened almond milk
- Ice cubes (optional)

Instructions:

1. In a blender, combine the fresh spinach leaves, cucumber slices, chopped green apple, ripe banana, non-fat Greek yogurt, chia seeds, and honey (if using).
2. Pour in the unsweetened almond milk to the blender.
3. If you prefer a colder smoothie, add a handful of ice cubes.
4. Blend on high speed until the mixture is smooth and creamy.
5. Stop the blender and scrape down the sides if needed, ensuring all ingredients are well combined.
6. Pour the green smoothie into glasses and serve immediately.
7. Garnish with a slice of cucumber or a sprinkle of chia seeds if desired.

Nutrition Information:
Per Serving
- Calories: 150, Total Fat: 3g, Saturated Fat: 0.5g, Cholesterol: 0mg, Sodium: 80mg, Total Carbohydrates: 27g, Dietary Fiber: 5g, Sugars: 15g, Protein: 7g
Note: Nutrition Information is approximate and may vary based on specific ingredients and brands used. Adjust the honey and yogurt quantities according to your taste preferences and Weight Watchers plan.

98. Spinach and Cheese Breakfast Quesadilla

Start your day on a healthy and delicious note with our Spinach and Cheese Breakfast Quesadilla. Packed with wholesome ingredients and bursting with flavor, this breakfast option is not only satisfying but also friendly to your Weight Watchers journey. The combination of spinach and cheese adds a nutritious punch, making it a perfect choice for those looking to enjoy a flavorful breakfast without compromising on their wellness goals.

Serving: Makes 2 quesadillas
Preparation Time: 10 minutes
Ready Time: 15 minutes

Ingredients:
- 4 whole wheat tortillas (8-inch diameter)
- 1 cup fresh spinach, chopped
- 1 cup reduced-fat shredded cheddar cheese

- 4 large eggs, beaten
- 1/2 cup diced tomatoes
- 1/4 cup diced red onion
- 1/4 cup diced bell peppers (any color)
- 1/2 teaspoon olive oil
- Salt and pepper to taste
- Optional toppings: salsa, Greek yogurt, or hot sauce

Instructions:
1. In a non-stick skillet, heat olive oil over medium heat. Add diced red onion and bell peppers, sautéing until softened.
2. Add chopped spinach to the skillet and cook until wilted. Season with salt and pepper to taste.
3. Push the vegetables to one side of the skillet and pour beaten eggs into the empty side. Scramble the eggs until fully cooked.
4. Remove the skillet from heat and mix the scrambled eggs with the sautéed vegetables.
5. On a separate griddle or skillet, place one whole wheat tortilla. Sprinkle half of the shredded cheddar cheese evenly over the tortilla.
6. Spoon half of the egg and vegetable mixture over the cheese, spreading it evenly.
7. Place a second tortilla on top, pressing down gently. Cook until the bottom tortilla is golden brown, then carefully flip the quesadilla and cook the other side until it's crispy and the cheese is melted.
8. Repeat the process for the second quesadilla.
9. Once both quesadillas are cooked, remove them from the griddle and let them cool for a minute before slicing into wedges.
10. Serve hot with diced tomatoes and your choice of optional toppings like salsa, Greek yogurt, or hot sauce.

Nutrition Information:
Per serving (1 quesadilla):
- Calories: 320, Total Fat: 16g, Saturated Fat: 6g, Cholesterol: 370mg, Sodium: 550mg, Total Carbohydrates: 26g, Dietary Fiber: 6g, Sugars: 2g, Protein: 20g

Enjoy this Spinach and Cheese Breakfast Quesadilla guilt-free as you embark on your Weight Watchers journey!

99. Baked Egg in Avocado

Start your day on a delicious and nutritious note with our Baked Egg in Avocado recipe—a perfect addition to your collection of Popular Weight Watchers Breakfast Recipes. Packed with protein, healthy fats, and a burst of flavor, this dish will keep you satisfied and energized throughout the morning. Indulge in a delightful combination of creamy avocado and perfectly baked eggs, creating a breakfast treat that's as wholesome as it is delicious.

Serving: 2 servings
Preparation Time: 10 minutes
Ready Time: 20 minutes

Ingredients:
- 2 ripe avocados
- 4 large eggs
- Salt and pepper, to taste
- Optional toppings: diced tomatoes, chopped cilantro, hot sauce

Instructions:
1. Preheat your oven to 425°F (220°C).
2. Cut the avocados in half and carefully scoop out a small portion of the flesh to create a well for the egg.
3. Place the avocado halves in a baking dish to prevent them from tipping over.
4. Crack one egg into each avocado half, ensuring not to overflow.
5. Season with salt and pepper to taste.
6. Bake in the preheated oven for approximately 15-20 minutes or until the eggs reach your desired level of doneness.
7. Remove from the oven and let them cool for a few minutes.
8. Sprinkle with optional toppings such as diced tomatoes, chopped cilantro, or a drizzle of hot sauce for an extra kick.
9. Serve immediately and enjoy the creamy goodness of Baked Egg in Avocado.

Nutrition Information:
Per serving (2 halves with eggs):
- Calories: 320, Protein: 12g, Fat: 26g, Carbohydrates: 12g, Fiber: 9g

Note: Nutrition Information may vary based on the size of avocados and specific toppings used.

100. Almond Joy Protein Shake

Start your day with a delicious and nutritious Almond Joy Protein Shake—a delightful blend of flavors reminiscent of the classic candy bar. Packed with the goodness of almonds, coconut, and chocolate, this protein shake is not only a tasty treat but also a fantastic way to kickstart your morning. Plus, it's a perfect addition to your Popular Weight Watchers Breakfast Recipes collection, helping you stay on track with your health and wellness goals.

Serving: 1 serving
Preparation Time: 5 minutes
Ready Time: 5 minutes

Ingredients:
- 1 cup unsweetened almond milk
- 1 scoop chocolate protein powder (ensure it fits your Weight Watchers plan)
- 2 tablespoons unsweetened shredded coconut
- 1 tablespoon almond butter
- 1/2 teaspoon almond extract
- 1/2 teaspoon coconut extract
- 1/2 teaspoon vanilla extract
- Ice cubes (optional)
- Sweetener of choice (optional, based on personal preference and Weight Watchers plan)

Instructions:
1. In a blender, combine the unsweetened almond milk, chocolate protein powder, unsweetened shredded coconut, almond butter, almond extract, coconut extract, and vanilla extract.
2. If you prefer a colder shake, add a handful of ice cubes to the blender.
3. Blend all the ingredients until smooth and creamy.
4. Taste the shake and add sweetener if desired, adjusting according to your personal preference and adherence to your Weight Watchers plan.

5. Pour the Almond Joy Protein Shake into a glass.
6. Garnish with a sprinkle of shredded coconut on top for an extra touch of flavor.
7. Enjoy your guilt-free and satisfying breakfast treat!

Nutrition Information:
Note: Nutritional values may vary based on specific ingredients used and individual preferences.
- Calories: Approximately 250 kcal, Protein: 25g, Fat: 15g, Carbohydrates: 8g, Fiber: 4g, Sugar: 1g
- Weight Watchers Points: X points (adjust based on your specific plan)

101. Peanut Butter and Jelly Overnight Oats

Jumpstart your day with a delicious and nutritious breakfast that's both satisfying and Weight Watchers-friendly. Our Peanut Butter and Jelly Overnight Oats are a delightful twist on a classic favorite. Packed with wholesome ingredients and the irresistible combination of peanut butter and jelly, this recipe will keep you energized and on track with your wellness goals. Make mornings easier with this simple, make-ahead meal that's as convenient as it is tasty.

Serving: 1 serving
Preparation Time: 10 minutes
Ready Time: Overnight (at least 6-8 hours of refrigeration)

Ingredients:
- 1/2 cup old-fashioned rolled oats
- 1/2 cup unsweetened almond milk (or your preferred milk)
- 1 tablespoon chia seeds
- 1 tablespoon powdered peanut butter
- 1/2 teaspoon vanilla extract
- 1 tablespoon sugar-free raspberry jam (or your favorite flavor)
- 1 tablespoon natural peanut butter
- Fresh berries for topping (optional)

Instructions:

1. In a mason jar or airtight container, combine the rolled oats, almond milk, chia seeds, powdered peanut butter, and vanilla extract. Mix well to ensure the ingredients are evenly distributed.
2. Spoon the sugar-free raspberry jam onto the oat mixture, and then add the natural peanut butter.
3. Stir gently to swirl the peanut butter and jelly into the oats without fully combining. This will create a delightful marbled effect.
4. Seal the jar or container and refrigerate overnight, or for at least 6-8 hours. This allows the oats to absorb the liquid and develop a creamy, pudding-like consistency.
5. Before serving, give the oats a good stir to combine all the flavors. If desired, top with fresh berries for an extra burst of sweetness and antioxidants.
6. Enjoy your Peanut Butter and Jelly Overnight Oats straight from the fridge or let them come to room temperature. Feel free to adjust the sweetness by adding more jam or peanut butter to suit your taste.

Nutrition Information:
- Calories: 350, Protein: 12g, Fat: 16g, Carbohydrates: 42g, Fiber: 10g, Sugar: 5g
- Weight Watchers SmartPoints: 8

Start your day right with this delightful Peanut Butter and Jelly Overnight Oats recipe that not only satisfies your cravings but also aligns with your wellness journey.

102. Breakfast Quiche with Spinach and Tomatoes

Start your day on a healthy and delicious note with our Breakfast Quiche featuring nutrient-rich spinach and vibrant tomatoes. This recipe is a perfect addition to your Weight Watchers journey, providing a satisfying and flavorful breakfast that won't compromise your wellness goals. Packed with protein and veggies, this quiche is a delightful way to kickstart your morning while staying on track with your Weight Watchers plan.

Serving: 4 servings
Preparation Time: 15 minutes
Ready Time: 45 minutes

Ingredients:
- 1 pre-made whole wheat pie crust
- 1 cup fresh spinach, chopped
- 1 cup cherry tomatoes, halved
- 1/2 cup red onion, finely chopped
- 1 cup reduced-fat shredded mozzarella cheese
- 4 large eggs
- 1 cup fat-free milk
- 1/2 teaspoon garlic powder
- 1/2 teaspoon onion powder
- Salt and pepper to taste

Instructions:
1. Preheat the oven to 375°F (190°C).
2. In a skillet over medium heat, sauté the chopped spinach, cherry tomatoes, and red onion until the vegetables are tender. Set aside to cool.
3. Roll out the whole wheat pie crust and press it into a pie dish, trimming any excess crust.
4. In a bowl, whisk together the eggs, fat-free milk, garlic powder, onion powder, salt, and pepper.
5. Spread the sautéed vegetables evenly over the pie crust. Sprinkle the shredded mozzarella cheese on top.
6. Pour the egg mixture over the vegetables and cheese.
7. Bake in the preheated oven for 30-35 minutes or until the quiche is set and the top is golden brown.
8. Allow the quiche to cool for a few minutes before slicing.

Nutrition Information
(per serving):
- Calories: 250, Total Fat: 12g, Saturated Fat: 4g, Cholesterol: 190mg, Sodium: 350mg, Total Carbohydrates: 20g, Dietary Fiber: 2g, Sugars: 2g, Protein: 15g

Note: Nutrition Information is approximate and may vary based on specific ingredients used. Adjust serving sizes accordingly to fit your Weight Watchers plan.

CONCLUSION

Smart Start Mornings: 102 Popular Weight Watchers Breakfast Recipes" offers a comprehensive and delicious array of breakfast options designed to support a healthy lifestyle with Weight Watchers principles. As we conclude this cookbook journey, it becomes evident that breakfast isn't just the first meal of the day; it's a pivotal moment where we set the tone for our nutritional choices and well-being.

Throughout this cookbook, we've explored a diverse range of recipes meticulously crafted to balance flavor, nutrition, and Weight Watchers SmartPoints. From hearty classics like oatmeal variations and egg dishes to innovative smoothies and baked goods, each recipe has been thoughtfully developed to cater to different tastes and dietary needs. The emphasis on smart ingredient choices and portion control not only enhances the culinary experience but also supports sustainable weight management goals.

One of the standout features of "Smart Start Mornings" is its ability to transform breakfast from a rushed necessity into a pleasurable and health-conscious ritual. By offering alternatives to traditional high-calorie options and highlighting the versatility of wholesome ingredients, this cookbook empowers readers to make informed choices that align with their wellness objectives.

Moreover, the practicality of the recipes ensures that they are accessible to cooks of all skill levels. Whether you're preparing a quick weekday meal or indulging in a leisurely weekend brunch, each dish is designed to be easy to follow, encouraging culinary exploration without intimidation.

Beyond the kitchen, "Smart Start Mornings" fosters a deeper appreciation for the role breakfast plays in overall health. By promoting balanced nutrition early in the day, the cookbook advocates for sustained energy levels, improved focus, and better appetite control throughout the day—

a holistic approach to wellness that extends far beyond the breakfast table.

In essence, "Smart Start Mornings: 102 Popular Weight Watchers Breakfast Recipes" is more than just a collection of recipes; it's a guide to embracing a healthier lifestyle through mindful eating. As you continue your journey towards wellness, may these recipes serve as a foundation for creating mornings filled with nourishment, satisfaction, and a renewed sense of vitality. Here's to starting each day with intention, and to the countless delicious possibilities that await as you explore the world of smart breakfast choices.

Printed in Great Britain
by Amazon